The Ethical Omnivore

Laura Dalrymple
Grant Hilliard
Feather and Bone

murdoch books
Sydney | London

Contents

Let's eat

*Recipes for conscientious carnivory
from friends of Feather and Bone*

Preface

Every day for the past 14 years, we've been answering questions in our butchery from people trying to come to terms with their relationship to meat. People who have a desire to do the 'right' thing (whatever that may be for them), but find the food production landscape opaque and confusing.

'Where does my meat come from?'
'How did it live?'
'How did it die?'
'What impact did it have on climate change?'
'What do the labels mean?'
'How do I cook it?'
'How much should I eat?'
'Should I eat meat at all?'

This book gives you our answers to these questions, with the goal of helping you to decide which food production systems you want to support. We're a partnership, so sometimes we tell our story in unison, and sometimes we speak alone.

We start deep in the soil and finish on the table and, along the way, we share our experiences, inspiring stories from our community, as well as recipes for eating the whole animal and not wasting a morsel.

We're unapologetically on the side of food production systems that foster sustainable biodiversity, resilience and vitality in soil, plant, animal and human communities. That might sound a bit vague and possibly self-evident, like saying you're on the side of good not evil, or that you don't support axe murderers. After all, who *wouldn't* support sustainable diversity, resilience and vitality?

Well, most of us, as it turns out. This isn't intentional, of course, but we've become so disengaged from the sources of our food that we mostly can't vouch for the way it was produced. In fact, when you look beyond the packaging, the truth is that most of the food we consume is over-processed, nutritionally compromised and produced out of an intensive, monocultural system that is dependent on external interventions. That system is intrinsically fragile — certainly not diverse, resilient and vital.

This is problematic in countless ways, not least of which are the consequences for human health. It turns out there's a direct link between the diversity and health of microbial life in the human gut and the diversity and microbial life in the soil in which our food grows, via the chain of plants and animals we consume. We are, literally, what our food ate. The broader the range of foods we eat and the broader the range of foods they ate, the more diverse our gut microbiome becomes, and the more resilient we are to physical and mental disease. It's not surprising that the exploding rate of inflammatory diseases, such as diabetes and dementia, correlates to the decline in the diversity of foods we eat and the attendant reduction in gut microbial diversity. (It's what we see at the butchery every day: more and more people coming in with chronic, inexplicable allergies, and inflammation and gut problems. Of course, they are a tiny percentage of the population, but they come to us because they're looking for clean food as medicine, and to us it looks like an epidemic.)

Incidentally, not only has the diversity of foods we eat declined, but we also don't cook and eat together as much as we did 50 years ago. Given that social interaction is a key predictor of good mental health, it's probably no accident that mental health problems are on the rise. (There you go, it's not only doing the crossword and learning how to tap dance that will help fend off dementia, it's cooking and eating together, too!)

When it comes to the way our food is produced, we do have a choice — we don't just have to swallow what's served up. We can start demanding more transparency and accountability from the people selling us our food — whether it's plant or animal-based — and spend our money supporting agricultural systems that match our views and beliefs. We can eat a little less meat with a little more provenance — and we can cook together more, gathering around the table and building our own diverse, resilient and vital communities.

Right: *Pasture-raised Berkshire Duroc weaner pigs at Extraordinary Pork, NSW. Extraordinary Pork run a very rare closed-loop system in which the heritage breed pigs' entire life cycle occurs on the farm — from birth to death. Read about them on page 76.*

*Pasture-raised
Berkshire Duroc weaner
pig at Extraordinary
Pork, NSW.*

Let's talk

*Texel flock at Moorlands
Bio-dynamic Farm, NSW.*

1.
We're all in this together

A filmmaker and a graphic designer walk into a butchery...

Far from being too small to make a difference, each of us is actually an intrinsic part of a dynamic and interconnected world that shifts and changes according to the actions of each element within it. We're all simultaneously more vulnerable and more powerful than we realise.

W e are all inextricably linked in a vast, natural community, and every step that each of us takes — no matter how large or small — towards a more considered and beneficial relationship with nature is good for everyone else.

You might think that's an odd way to start a book written by butchers — but over the past 14 years we've learned that the food we eat, whether it's from animals or plants, must be understood as the embodiment of the system in which it was produced. So if you're swallowing that system and making it part of yours, then it better be good for your body and your conscience.

'Regenerative agriculture' describes a system of agricultural management practices designed to increase biodiversity, enrich soil, capture carbon, improve the water cycle, increase resilience in the face of climate instability, and break the cycle of diminishing returns that is at the heart of the conventional agricultural system's dependency on expensive, external inputs.

The benefits of regenerative farming ripple far beyond the boundary fence, spreading through the fungi and microbes in the soil, up and down through plant roots and stems, into the systems of all the creatures living and dying above the surface of the soil, including us — no matter how far removed we might be from the original source of our food.

Left: Farmers Michael and Alexandra Hicks discussing the 2019 drought with one of their Berkshire sows at Extraordinary Pork, NSW.

This may not be front of mind when you're tucking into your dinner every night. But if you stop, fork halfway to your mouth, to really question how your food is produced and where it comes from, no matter how opaque or convoluted the journey from source to fork might be, it soon becomes clear that every living thing is connected by this natural web of transmission. We are all inextricably linked in a vast, natural community, and every step that each of us takes — no matter how large or small — towards a more considered and beneficial relationship with nature is good for everyone else. This is the most important thing we've learned, the thing that continues to shape and colour our world.

We've been lucky enough to spend a lot of time on farms being educated about holistic farming by some of the best in Australia. The regenerative work done by these farmers is often transformative, and their dogged determination to build resilient, fertile ecosystems is making a critical contribution to the long-term sustainability of the country. Not just for their little patch but for all of us, wherever we live. It might seem a stretch to suggest that the actions of a farmer in one location have an impact on other people living in the next district, or even in another country. But the behaviours that contribute to the reduction in capacity that we see across the spectrum, from declining soil fertility and species loss to the hollowing out of rural communities, are common across the world and affect all of us. Every time any one of us, producer or consumer (or both), takes a step to mitigate against this destructive behaviour, we are improving the entire planet's prospects.

We've admired animals on pasture and later received them in our cool room, translating the story that the whole carcass tells us about the health and vitality of the animals and the ecosystem in which they lived, and passing that information back to the farmers who raised them and on to the customers who eat them.

We've wrestled with the moral ambiguity of raising animals for slaughter and learned that everything we eat, whether it's animal or plant-derived, comes out of a cycle of life and death.

We've come to understand that the best-quality produce always comes from farms that are managed as ecosystems of communities of interdependent species. The more we've learned, the more aghast we are at the destruction wrought by the extraction-based model of intensive agriculture, and all the more determined to pursue and support the work of producers who are regenerating their farms and building diversity, fertility and resilience for the long term.

Most of us are blissfully unaware of — or choose to gloss over — the fact that the choices we make at the checkout determine the way animals are raised, and how the environments in which they live are managed. We've been infantilised by a lack of information, and that's worked very well for the half-dozen multinational conglomerates who own the production, distribution and sale of most of the food in the world. For them, the less we know about how our food is produced, and the more unquestioningly we consume it, the better.

But it isn't working very well for any of us — the end consumer, the farmer, or the natural world on which we depend. In some parts of the world, we're starving to death; in others, we're suffering from obesity and diabetes epidemics and chronic food intolerance problems. The intensive monocultural system that produces most of our food is contributing to species extinction, loss of capacity and antibiotic resistance. Things are critically out of balance, and it's time for all of us to take back control over the choices we make.

Take food labelling. We found that the more we tried to decipher what all the labels attached to meat and poultry actually meant, the more indignant we became about how intentionally misleading they are. Food retailing is awash with seductive claims that prey on the good intentions of consumers, such as the farcical certification that allows 10,000 chickens housed in a fixed shed sitting on a hectare of land to be called 'free range'. (See page 22 for more about that.)

Bemused and irritated by all the double-speak designed to dumb down the facts and pacify concerned but time-poor consumers, we decided there was room for a straightforward butchery committed to guaranteed provenance and whole-animal consumption. So, we built a business around supply chain transparency, offering a clear line of sight from the farm to the consumer, providing as much guidance as we could to enable more informed choices and help to navigate the tricky questions that come with eating animals.

Terroir and testicles

You might be surprised to see these two words sharing the same sentence and, until fairly recently, so would we. We didn't set out to build a butchery. In fact, we didn't set out to be butchers at all. There we were, quite happily tootling along together on our perfectly satisfactory, unrelated career paths, when suddenly we veered wildly off course and plunged headlong into the perils of running a small butchery business with no prior experience or skill at all. What lunatic would plan that?

We agree that it's all Grant's fault, at that time an aspiring filmmaker working in restaurants as a manager and sommelier. About 15 years ago, it began to dawn on him there was something peculiar about the fact that wines were justly fussed over for their pedigree, genetics and terroir, but meat was largely generic, regardless of the breed or production method or place. With a burgeoning interest in sustainable agriculture, a passion for artisan culture and a courage borne of ignorance, he found some farmers growing rare breeds of sheep and some chefs willing to buy their lambs … and, lo and behold, 'Feather and Bone — Rare Breed Providore and Whole Animal Butchery' was born. A few years later, Laura was lured into the business and added marketing and project management to Grant's filmmaking and hospitality skills, to round out a devastatingly pertinent business skill set. Things were looking good.

Even from the outset, as we blundered our way through the first steps in our butchery and farming education, we had a glimmering sense of the importance of the concept of natural networks, so we searched for farmers who were prioritising a long-term, holistic philosophy. Aside from the positive impacts on human, animal and environmental welfare of this approach, we also found that the produce from these farms was head and shoulders above anything else in quality and flavour. It was easy to be inspired by the challenge

Let's talk

of convincing other people that they should be supporting these beneficial production systems, too. So we developed some guiding principles that have formed the bedrock of our business (see page 246 for the full list).

In a nutshell, we source everything directly from the farmer, and we visit all the farms from which we source, which gives us a rich understanding of what we're selling. Unlike most butchers who buy boxes of boned meat containing only the parts of the animal they know they can sell, we buy all of our meat on the bone — no boxed meat. Whole-animal butchery ensures traceability to the paddock, provides a wealth of information about the animal and the condition of the farm, allows for dry-ageing parts of the carcass, offers the full range of different muscles and cuts available, and also encourages consumers to expand their culinary repertoire and reclaim lost cooking skills. It also enforces a no-waste approach. The animals we buy are raised outside on pasture, and all ruminants are pasture-fed and finished.

Opposite top: *Clara Bateman checking her Black Angus calves, South Hill Farm, NSW. Read about South Hill Farm on page 39.*

Opposite bottom: *80-year-old Tony Franckin with Euan, the 15-year-old Hereford bull that sires the vealers Tony supplies to us from Franckin's biodynamic farm near Comboyne, NSW. Not many farmers and bulls are this relaxed and calm together. In the 80s, Tony and his wife, Josie, pioneered Australian portable chicken shelters for free-range egg production and their pasture-raised chickens were fed a mix of organic, home-milled grains and seaweed soaked in biodynamic milk from their dairy. Not a bad life for a chicken. Or a bull.*

As well as informing the way we run our business, these principles have determined the kinds of people we seek out and who we choose to work with. We've been fortunate to partner with a fascinating range of producers who found the agricultural status quo wanting and who had the courage and foresight to strike out on a different path, determined to find a better way to work in harmony with the land. Whether these relationships are the result of dumb luck, good judgement or an excess of naive enthusiasm on our part is unclear, but there's no doubt that throwing yourself sideways into something and following an unconventional route can lead to some wonderfully surprising and rewarding outcomes and relationships.

Initially, we were very focused on genetic diversity and rare breeds, identifying ourselves, rather self-importantly, as the 'Rare Breed Providores'. This focus on provenance and breeds led us to quickly realise that we couldn't properly represent or promote a product or grower unless we'd been to the farm, met the farmer and understood it for ourselves. But, the more farms we visited and the more we learned, the more it dawned on us that heritage breeds were just one part of the picture.

We've spent many hours, in all sorts of weather and in all seasons, kneeling in paddocks examining manure, grasses and clods of soil while passionate regenerative farmers expound knowledgeably and tirelessly about soil microbes and rhizospheres. Often, we've done our farm trips in winter school holidays when we could more easily take time off work and haul our three sons along with us. After the first few experiences of nodding politely as we struggled to prevent fratricide, absorb the farmers' soil lessons and avoid frostbite, the penny started to drop and we began augmenting the field trips with our own studies about

soil, regenerative agriculture, genetic diversity and extensive livestock farming. Our bedside tables disappeared under piles of books as we cast the net wide and collected anything that looked useful. Every night in bed we would pore over the latest books and read the most interesting bits out loud.

It might have been the night that Grant chose to share the salient details about testicle dimensions from a cattle-breeding manual featuring a gallery of photographs of bull testicles that we began to wonder if we had crossed some kind of line in our eagerness to pay due respect to our work. It gave us pause, but it didn't dampen our enthusiasm, and we soon found we were getting almost as feverish about soil as the farmers with whom we work.

The more we've learned about soil, plants, animals and farming, the more we've come to understand that animals, rare breed or not, are just one component of an extensive, natural system, which is only as strong as

Above left: Biodynamic sheep farmer and endangered fish protector, Vince Heffernan at Moorlands Biodynamic Farm, NSW. Read more about Moorlands and the fish sanctuary on page 46.

Above centre: Buffalo dairy farmer Andrei Swegen shows off the pristine lakes that border his coastal farm. Read about Burraduc Farm's compassionate dairy model on page 54.

the health of its component parts. From the complex world of fungi and microbes in the soil, through to the insects and animals that live in and above it, every farm is a rich community of diverse, interconnected creatures, constantly responding and reacting to each other. You can't really focus on one element, such as animal welfare, without considering the welfare of everything else in the environment in which that animal lives, because one impacts the other and vice versa. Take that a step in the other direction, and you realise that you can't really think about animal welfare without thinking about the end consumer as well, because, once again, everything is connected.

Every time we buy something, we vote for the system that produced that product. If you don't understand the system, you've got no idea what you're supporting. Take free-range chicken eggs, for example.

The free-range chicken farce

Any sensible person reading the words 'free range' on a box of eggs would envisage a flock of chickens ranging free outside on pasture. After all, you can't range free inside a shed, can you? Well, as it turns out, under the current Australian Free Range Egg Labelling Standard legislation, you can.

It all came about because consumers began to demand a better animal welfare standard to that of the caged-egg industry. This was a good thing for the farmers who were already growing egg chickens in a way that would accord with the average punter's image of 'free range'— low stocking densities, mobile shelters and chickens moving at will across fresh pasture. However, it wasn't long before the large companies running intensive, caged-egg chicken operations that dominated the industry decided they wanted a piece of the free-range frittata, and soon the market was flooded with dubious product claims that couldn't be easily verified by consumers and, lacking the clout of the big operators, the genuine free-range growers found themselves sorely disadvantaged. It became clear that industry self-regulation wasn't working and that an independent standard was required. After a long battle during which the influence of the handful of dominant egg producers held sway, a Free Range Egg Labelling Standard was legislated that allows for a permanent stocking density of 10,000 birds per hectare — 6.6 times the maximum of 1500 birds per hectare that the pasture-based egg growers proposed.

It's true that there are doors on the sides of the fixed sheds at Free Range-certified egg farms that allow chickens access to the surrounding fields during daylight hours. And it's true that 10,000 birds per hectare makes for a convincingly reasonable-sounding stocking density of one bird per square metre. But you'd only achieve that ratio if all the birds were spread out evenly across the combined shed and field area, and those 10,000 birds included thousands of intrepid explorers willing to brave the vast expanses of open, unprotected territory to reach the perimeter fence. There are no protective shepherds or sheep dogs to fend off foxes or raptors at these farms. In practice, if the chickens' food, water and nesting boxes are inside the shed, and if the area outside their shed doesn't include shelter and compelling food

'Every time we buy something, we vote for the system that produced it.'

prospects, then, while they may range a short distance outside, they don't venture too far.

Instead, the majority of birds spend the majority of each day inside the shed, or within 10 metres or so of the shed, which gives you a real, constant stocking density of about 10–13 birds per square metre. Which would be tricky if they all decided to flap their wings at once. Anyone who's had anything to do with chickens will also tell you that it would only take a few days for a big flock of industrious hens to turn a well-vegetated area into a dust bowl, so the areas outside the fixed sheds are unlikely to be lush with plant and insect life. Inside the shed, the manure piles up and creates a significant waste problem.

There's no doubt that this system is vastly preferable to caged-egg production in which birds are permanently housed in cages inside sheds, but the images suggested by the term 'free range' and the truth are substantially different.

By contrast, a 'pasture-raised' chicken production system for both meat and egg-producing chickens is characterised by mobile roosting and laying shelters that are moved onto fresh pasture every few days. This prevents build-up of manure in any one location and distributes it across the pastures, turning the costly waste problem that occurs with fixed sheds into a free fertility boon for the pastures. Regularly moving to fresh pasture provides the chickens with constant fresh green pick, expanded foraging opportunities and new territories to explore, all of which translates into improved health and welfare outcomes.

However, the difficult truth is that healthy chickens that are raised outside on pasture, responding to the seasons and permitted to behave according to their natural instincts, generally do not produce eggs as consistently as chickens that are housed in sheds. We've become increasingly conditioned to having all food varieties on tap, regardless of the season, but consistent production and availability is a relatively new phenomenon, and only possible with a lot of unnatural interventions and costly, energy-hungry storage and distribution networks.

In fact, all natural systems are punctuated by periods of abstinence or pause to rest and restore. Most living creatures experience periods of growth

and dormancy in their natural life cycle. Humans are no exception, which is why fasting is a consistent feature of most human cultures.

For chickens, the urge to lay an egg is triggered by the pineal gland responding to light entering the eye. Left to their own devices, even chickens bred specifically to reliably pump out an egg a day won't lay in the shortest days of winter or when they're moulting, which is why producers use artificially lit sheds that maintain a consistent, optimum 16 hours of light. But every intervention comes with a cost. Short-circuiting a chicken's biological cycle and tricking her into laying every day produces a consistent supply of eggs, but it also prevents the chance to rest and recover, and reduces the overall productive life of the chicken. Think about it this way: an average commercial egg-laying chicken weighs about 2 kilograms, and in less than a month, a chicken externalises its total body weight in eggs. It's a big effort, and explains why egg chickens need a high-protein diet — and a bit of time off, occasionally. But in the intensive-farming lexicon, time off is lost production, wasted money and missed opportunity.

In a marketplace that values volume, speed and price over quality, animal welfare and environmental impact, there is a compelling reason for egg

Above: Farmer Brown's egg hens foraging, hunting, scratching, sheltering, dust bathing and generally doing what comes naturally. In the distance, their food and water trailers sit next to the mobile roosting shelters that are moved to fresh pasture every few days.

producers to contain their chickens, despite the costs involved. And when consumers begin questioning the ethics of conventional, intensive production methods and search for different options, it's not surprising that these same producers will do their darndest to dress up the so-called 'free range' standard as a vision of ecstatic, liberated chickens gambolling across verdant pastures.

Back at the supermarket shelf, there's a deafening cacophony of labels trumpeting feel-good motherhood statements, but an eerie silence when you search for the facts that support the claims. As well as 'free range' there are a host of other egg claims to decipher — 'organic', 'organic free range', 'eco-organic free range', 'free range natural living extra', 'natural living free range', 'nature's intention', 'cage free', 'cage-free liberty', 'corn-fed', 'barn-laid' and 'pasture-raised'. What do they all actually mean? The only thing that's abundantly clear is that this proliferation of appealing labels is a direct response to escalating consumer concern about animal and environmental welfare, and a lack of effective labelling regulation.

So, come back when you've separated the propaganda from the facts and you know exactly what all those terms really mean. You get double points if the people selling you the eggs can explain the difference between each label, and triple points if the producers themselves agree to let you onto their farm to see it for yourself. Our bet is that the retailers won't know much more than you do, and large producers will fob you off with excuses about biosecurity risks. When we've finished de-mystifying egg labelling, we'll start on meat chickens and work our way through the rest of the meat categories …

Fortunately for you and me, the birds and the landscape, a growing number of farmers are choosing the pastured model in which flocks of chickens genuinely range free on mixed pastures, moving with their mobile shelters every few days, and fertilising and improving the land as they go. In some cases, mixed farms use egg chickens to follow the pigs or cattle, because their industrious scratching and foraging helps to break down and scatter manure and keep insect populations in check. After the chooks, the pastures are left for long periods to allow the manure to break down into the soil and the vegetation to regenerate. It's an ideal, time-worn agricultural practice of using animals to work on our behalf in a way that's beneficial and productive for the entire system.

There's no denying that it costs more to produce eggs this way, and the retail price can be off-putting to many. But you might decide that, on balance, you'd prefer to eat a few less eggs if it means that you can choose to eat eggs produced by vigorous, healthy, pasture-raised chickens in a system that adds fertility to the land, and provides a sustainable income for the farmer.

Or you might even decide to join a community garden with a flock of chickens, or get a few backyard hens of your own, reducing your household waste by recycling your kitchen scraps for a regular supply of delicious, fresh eggs. (The economics of egg farming only allow for consistent production, which means there are always lots of 2-year-old, unemployed layer hens looking for a new home.) Chickens are also excellent free labour when it comes to turning over garden beds — and good company when you're hanging out the washing!

No man is an island

Over a decade spent operating as a whole-animal butchery at the busy intersection of production and consumption has given us the opportunity to see in many directions — and it has taught us that nothing is ever simply black or white. We've learned a lot about genetics, soil, poo and plants, and how to sell beef heart to a customer who wants sirloin. We've worked with scores of farmers who have prioritised long-term, sustainable fertility over short-term gains; to us their grit, imagination and commitment redefines the very idea of resilience. We've worked with professional chefs with the wit and curiosity to prioritise provenance over convenience, seeking produce that comes from suppliers who have a transparent commitment to sustainable practices, even when these natural systems promise less predictability and might cost a little more.

Our staff — unconventional people willing to be part of our unconventional journey — have challenged, supported and helped shape the business. Our retail customers come from all walks of life, drawn to us for a multitude of reasons, ranging from the promise of superior quality and our supply chain transparency, through to the search for clean food in an effort to improve conditions from autism and allergies to autoimmune diseases and anorexia. Whether they are flush with cash or eking out the money from payday to payday, or whether they eat meat once a day or once a month, their willingness to engage with hard questions and pursue a more balanced, compassionate footprint is inspiring.

We've watched small groups, organisations and community initiatives spring up and multiply over the past 10 years, all dedicated to promoting one aspect or another of sustainable food production and consumption. So often they're driven by passionate volunteers whose lives are already like over-stuffed suitcases, but who still manage to squeeze a bit more in because they're so energised by the cause.

All of these people — the producers, the co-workers, the customers, the activists — are part of our local community, and we've found that our position at the intersection of these groups has allowed us to link people, share information and open up the lines of sight between producers and consumers. Globally, there is a growing network of concerned individuals searching for authenticity, transparency and sustainable solutions that foster resilient communities and ecosystems. We are proud to be part of this thriving movement, and we are wildly excited by the potential.

Because, what all these people have taught us is that, no matter how far we might be from the sources of our food or how many steps it took to reach our table, we're all responsible for the ecosystems that produce our food.

It might seem obvious to many, but for us, really absorbing the simple idea that the physical universe is a network of thousands of interconnected communities — only one of which is our human community — has had a profound impact. Instead of seeing nature as a separate entity, an infinite resource for humans to exploit, we see now that we are actually indivisible from nature. This shift in perspective has been an unfolding revelation that has reverberated through our lives and magnified the importance of making choices that lead to healthier communities.

We instinctively understand this concept in relation to our own species. We know that we need each other. 'No man is an island entire of itself' wrote the English poet John Donne back in 1623 — and, as it turns out, nor is any microbe or fungus or plant or insect or animal. Far from being too small to make a difference, each of us is actually an intrinsic part of a dynamic and connected world that shifts and changes according to the actions of each element within it. We're all simultaneously more vulnerable *and* more powerful than we realise. Growing and making food isn't something that happens off stage, and over which we have no control. Every time you open your wallet or your mouth to eat, you're making a choice to support one production system or another, and every choice you make ripples back to the source and influences the production of your food. Every step that occurs in that system eventually loops back to you — to us. The question is, what sort of communities and ecosystems do we want to live in, and how do our choices make them happen?

Whether we like it or not, we are all intimately connected — the bee and the flower it visited yesterday, the cow and the grass she ate today, and you and me and the meal we'll share tomorrow.

We're all in this together.

2.
Never bare the earth

Stories from the soil

Whether it's a cow or a carrot, if you're eating something that depended on and absorbed the qualities of the soil on or in which it lived, then by extension you are also eating that soil.

I t took us a few years to get it, but we soon learned that it all starts with soil. Everything we eat, regardless of how it was produced, is inextricably connected to the earth, whether it's a potato or a pork chop.

Left: *The farmers with whom we work are as proud of their healthy soil and the rich diversity of plants in their pastures as they are of the product they send to market. Organic Wagyu farmer Rob Lennon is no exception. See page 40 for more on Rob.*

Your food might have been grown in an extensive system: the potato rooting down into soil rich with humus and pulsing with life; and the pig roaming on pasture, free to express its instincts to root, dig, graze and nest, its manure naturally fertilising the ground as it goes.

Or it might have been grown intensively: the potato lodged in sand rather than soil (because of consumers' apparent distaste for 'dirty' potatoes caked with earth); and the pig living with hundreds of others in a shed, fed a preventive medicated diet, creating huge amounts of waste that requires extensive treatment before being fit to be dispersed back into the soil as fertiliser. (In nature, there is no such thing as a waste management problem. Everything is consumed and absorbed to support more life.) Either way, it all starts and finishes with soil.

This seems sort of self-evident, we know. Whatever the system, most food is grown in or on the soil on farms. But what does that really mean?

Across the world, agricultural communities are contracting as the pressures of intensive production methods catering to a globalised food market squeeze out small farmers and give way to larger operators and more highly mechanised production systems. Farmers are ageing, their numbers are dwindling, and rural towns are suffering as younger generations who might once have forged a life on the land move to urban centres to pursue opportunities. Corporations don't put down roots and build community the way family farmers do. The connections that once existed between rural and urban citizens are breaking down as our cities swell and rural communities contract. As well as the reduction in empathy and understanding that results from any relationship breakdown, urban disconnection from rural production means consumers are increasingly ignorant about the way agriculture works. For example, a recent survey of Australian high school students revealed that the majority of them thought cotton came from an animal. Cotton, as you know, comes from a plant. It's also very telling when the major daily news outlets use photos of egg-producing chickens to illustrate stories about meat chickens, which happens often enough to be disconcerting. This separation from the source of our food makes us easy pickings for anyone making false claims about provenance. If you don't understand something, it's harder to distinguish between fact and fiction, which makes it easier to be duped into buying something produced in a way you might not support, and it also lets you off the hook. After all, you can't be held responsible for something if you don't know anything about it, right?

When we started digging for information, we realised that an understanding of soil was the crucial starting point for answering these questions about where our food, particularly our meat, comes from.

At first, inspired by Grant's experience of discovering the fascinating genetic diversity and complexity of the world of wine, we were convinced that the world of meat must hold the same promise and rewards, so we set off in pursuit of heritage or rare breeds. We were looking for producers who were fostering critical genetic diversity and premium quality within a sustainable farming practice, and we wanted to bring this eye-opening and mouth-watering offering to our customers (more about that in the next chapter).

But the more farms we visited, the more perplexed we became. It seemed that, almost without exception, the overriding focus for these sustainably managed farms wasn't the wonderful animals they were growing to sell for meat. Despite being passionate about their animals, the thing that really seemed to matter to the farmers was the condition of their *soil,* and the pastures on which their animals lived. This, they explained, was the well-spring for the health of everything on the farm. Fostering healthy soil was what they considered to be their real work.

Overgrazing, overcropping and excessive land-clearing — widespread practices in Australia, which holds the dubious honour of being among the top 10 global leaders in deforestation, and the only developed nation on the list — jeopardise soil health and the long-term prospects of the entire ecosystem, including the animals or plants being raised for food. So this focus on soil health makes sense.

Even so, the idea that a farmer might be as interested in the condition of their soil as they are in the condition of the cattle that provide their income, tips conventional wisdom on its head. We began to see that, instead of organising the farm entirely around the product that goes to market, these farmers see the thing they sell as simply one expression — albeit a very important one —

of the ecosystem of the farm. This focus on soil and the rich life within it is an anchor point that all the farmers we work with have in common, and it dictates the way they manage their farms. It forces a long-term view, brings the connections between all creatures into stark relief, and prompts an unconventional appreciation of value.

Traditionally, land is valued by the size of the surface area — the square kilometres marked on a map. But a regenerative farmer pursuing holistic farm health moves beyond a two-dimensional approach to value, and extends the picture to include all the activity that happens under the ground as well. A farm's productive capacity springs from the soil, so the *condition* of the soil becomes a key measure of value. In fact, if the soil and the whole farm ecosystem is thriving, regenerative farmers find that even when areas of a farm are taken out of productivity and allowed to rest and recover for prolonged periods, it is possible to increase the overall productivity of the farm, over and above what is produced when the entire area of the farm is working but at a lower capacity. It's an odd paradox that working less land could actually produce more capacity. But if a farmer's management practice results in an increase of average topsoil cover from, say, 20 centimetres to 30 centimetres, then the farmer has effectively added the potential to increase productivity by a whopping 50 per cent. Applying this kind of three-dimensional perspective allows for an entirely different way of understanding value and capacity. Maybe, in the future, factors such as carbon sequestration and species diversity will become part of the mainstream value calculation. (In fact, there are certification standards being developed now that are seeking to do just that.)

The marriage between heaven and earth

Jerry Brunetti, an influential biological agri-consultant, called soil the 'marriage between heaven and earth' — which makes total sense when you understand a bit about what's happening under the ground and how lively soil creates capacity.

Healthy soil is a rich, spongey, sweet-smelling universe filled with tiny pockets of air and water that create the conditions for life. Hundreds of communities of different creatures, from fungi and microbes to insects and plants, live in the soil, all busily engaged in symbiotic exchanges of energy, nutrients and information. As Brunetti explains, create the conditions for any living thing to thrive and you'll see a corresponding escalation in complexity, allowing for greater opportunities for biological activity and exchange. The more diverse the life in the soil, the more dynamic the interchanges, and the greater the benefits for everything living above and below the soil. Everything has a purpose, every death provides food and fosters creation, and there is as much cooperation as there is competition.

Excessive and continuous application of fertilisers, for example, might speed up output and produce abundance in the short term, but over time, they undermine the symbiotic relationships between soil microbes and plants, and drastically reduce resilience and weaken the soil. It's an extractive system of diminishing returns that is reminiscent of the mining industry. Put simply, healthy soils depend on a constant and lively exchange of energy, nutrients and minerals between fungi, microbes and plants. But excessive application of an external fertiliser provides free minerals and nutrients so plants don't have to trade energy with the microbes. Without a viable trading partner, the microbes dissipate, the life and vitality of the ecosystem is depleted, the plants are hooked on an external fix, and it requires increasing amounts of fertilisers to maintain and boost fertility.

As research methods develop, we're discovering previously unimaginable things about the way subterranean communities of microbes and fungi operate, and it makes these interventions seem increasingly unwise and misdirected. While plants don't have a brain or nervous system, plant behaviour is much more sophisticated, complex and self-determining than we'd previously realised. Whether in your garden, in a forest or in fields of crops, plants are constantly communicating with each other, sharing resources and making choices that further their survival and prosperity. For example, trees and fungi enjoy a symbiotic relationship in which networks of fungi wrap around and between tree roots, receiving sugars from the trees and, in exchange, acting as subterranean transmitters, allowing information to pass between trees to aid in keeping communities of trees safe and healthy. It turns out that the organisation and interplay of subterranean organisms is much more complex than we'd previously understood, and the evidence is piling up to show that the interventionist strategies employed in industrial agricultural systems in pursuit of short-term productivity are blunt weapons that wreak havoc on soil biomes.

Regenerative farmers argue that the smartest thing farmers can do is to recognise and encourage nature's superior ability to self-organise and create capacity.

Is it spongey?

Within soil, most of the action occurs in the top 13 centimetres or so, the precious 'topsoil' that plays a critical role in plant growth and determines the soil's sponginess — its capacity to retain water and store carbon. In fact, the word 'spongey' was frequently used by European explorers to describe the Australian grasslands when they first arrived over 200 years ago, and it's a perfect description of the slightly bouncy sensation of walking across

Above: *At Moorlands Biodynamic Farm, sixth-generation sheep farmer Vince Heffernan has spent 20 years regenerating his ancestral country in an effort to restore some of the resilience and species diversity that would have existed here when his forebears first arrived.* Read more on page 46.

Never bare the earth

a healthy landscape carpeted with plants rooted in soil that's packed with life. In his book *Dark Emu*, Bruce Pascoe quotes G.T. Lloyd, western Victoria's first European settler, as saying his horses sank to their fetlocks into the soil, as if it were sponge. That was around 1830. It's a sorry comment on the way we've managed the country since then that so much of that spongey, fertile grassland is now denuded, compacted and comatose.

The more we saw and learned, the more we realised that the farms on which the animals in our cool rooms had lived are regenerative oases in a scarred farming landscape that has, since European settlement, largely been managed with tools and systems designed for younger European ecosystems with plentiful water and fertile, volcanic soils. Australia is isolated, ancient and dry, with a unique flora and fauna, and it couldn't be more different to the places from which these management practices derive. Despite the evidence — gaping chasms caused by erosion, dust storms, inexplicable die-back, increased soil salinity, more extreme weather events with slower recovery periods — generations of farmers have ploughed on with a blind faith in these systems and a spiralling addiction to the chemicals required to ameliorate the damage and maintain viable outputs. Farmers get poorer, land is depleted, species are lost — and the only winners are the chemical manufacturers.

Australians, like most people, are territorial and proud and fiercely guard the right to independently manage their patch, whether it's a farm or a suburban plot. Indigenous Australians managed the land according to the rule that the ecosystem is a universal resource to be protected by all for the good of all. This unifying belief dictated common land management strategies that ensured that all life flourished, from one end of the country to the other. But this approach is long gone. When we travel across the country visiting the farms we represent, the difference in farm management strategies is abundantly clear. We've visited around 100 farms over the years and, almost without exception, they do not share the same management approach as their neighbours. Everything changes at the fence line.

While self-determination is each farmer's legal right, there is mounting environmental evidence that this individualistic approach might not be

'It's time for a land management approach that prioritises custodial responsibility for the benefit of all.'

working as well as we'd like and is, in fact, causing irreparable damage to our collective long-term prosperity. When the differences in land management and the outcomes are as stark as we see today, it's hard not to conclude that maybe what's needed now is a review of these ideas of territory and individuality. It's idealistic, we know, but maybe it's time to return to an approach that prioritises custodial responsibility for the benefit of all?

Blowing in the wind

Deprived of life, soil becomes inert — simply dirt. One of the tangible symptoms of this issue is the increasingly common dirt storms that whip up the exposed topsoil from southern Queensland down to northern Victoria, carrying it off and blanketing city cars with a fine silt, depositing it in the Tasman Sea and as far away as mountain ranges in New Zealand. While drought is often the trigger for these dirt storms, the underlying instigators are excessive cultivation and/or overgrazing. Both lead to either complete or near complete destruction of groundcover. Without groundcover to protect and feed the life below — and without the roots, fungi and microbes to hold the soil together and facilitate the critical exchanges of energy, nutrients and information — the exposed dirt, desiccated by drought, is free to fly. And fly it does, taking years to rebuild — and only then if the plant communities that hold it in place are re-established. Even dead grasses play a vital role in helping to nurture, stabilise and insulate the soil, and reduce evaporation.

Dirt storms caused by agricultural mismanagement are by no means a new or uniquely Australian phenomenon. In 1977, southern California experienced the Great Bakersfield Dust Storm, attributed to extended drought coupled with agricultural practices that turned soil into loose, bare dirt. It's likely that some of those affected by this storm were the children or grandchildren of the estimated 2.5 million people who had arrived in California in the mid 1930s — blow-ins from the 'dust bowl' centred on the Great Plains states of Kansas, Oklahoma and northern Texas, who with the wind at their backs, were pushed west from the desolation of dust-drifts deep enough to bury houses and destroy communities. This was the largest exodus caused by preventable environmental degradation the modern world has ever known, and it's hard to grasp how a calamity of that scale could occur.

For many thousands of years until the 1920s, the grasslands of the Great Plains had mostly been used for grazing, seasonally hosting a fair proportion of the estimated 50 million–strong bison migration that made the annual pilgrimage from north to south, following the season and forage. Over centuries, as the bison moved rapidly across the plains, the plants and animals had evolved symbiotic, mutually beneficial relationships that allowed the ecosystem to thrive and survive. Astonishingly, after European settlement, it took little more than 150 years for the bison population to be counted in the hundreds, while in most cases their domesticated relatives — the sons and daughters of Bos Taurus cattle of Europe — had taken their place.

However, following World War I, despite the low rainfall in the area, grazing was largely replaced by cropping, and millions of acres of these valuable grasslands were ploughed under in order to grow thirsty wheat. This decision proved disastrous when, little more than a decade later, a sustained dry period stretching from the late 1920s through to the early 1930s caused catastrophic agricultural failure, and dramatically rearranged the social, environmental and cultural landscape of the American Midwest. The precious balance achieved by co-efficient and geographically appropriate plant and animal communities that had lasted for thousands of years was wiped out by an irresponsible lack of observation and long-term vision.

Leaving money in the paddock

In intensive farming, the idea that you would create a network of small paddocks; frequently and laboriously rotate your animals across your pastures (cell-grazing); 'rest' paddocks for many months at a time, thereby always ensuring a protective layer of vegetation in the paddock and not using it all for fodder — it's considered nonsensical. It's dismissed as 'leaving money in the paddock'. Instead, keeping animals in one place and allowing them to graze the pasture down to the ground is seen as a sensible use of existing resources, particularly in drought conditions when there's so little fodder that wasting anything seems irresponsible. Except, once the plants are gone and the earth is exposed, there is a rapid loss of moisture and organic matter, the communities of creatures that hold the soil together dissipate and the battle to restore vegetation is long and arduous. In a sustainable system, up to 40 per cent of the carbon that grasses photosynthesise is pushed out to feed the soil and

Above: *Grass roots farming: a stark illustration of the contrast in management practices between two neighbouring farms, both affected by long-term drought. On the right, the vegetation is grazed to the roots, leaving the soil exposed, unprotected and vulnerable. On the left, grass roots knit the topsoil in place, preventing evaporation, feeding and protecting the soil.*

keep it healthy in a mutually beneficial relationship. But overgrazed or over-cultivated land, stripped of vegetation, cannot feed the soil and the ground becomes compacted and inhospitable, unable to absorb carbon and water, air and light or allow roots to permeate. Definitely not 'spongey'. So, the grass may represent money left in the paddock — but it's money well spent if it means a faster recovery and long-term security.

Clara Bateman, a cattle farmer who has spent 20 years regenerating her beautiful 40-acre farm, South Hill, in the famously lush and fertile Southern Highlands just south of Sydney, tells a cautionary but hopeful tale about soil management. During the Millennium Drought, the local energy company was attempting to replace a steel stanchion with foundations on both sides of the fence between Clara's and her neighbour's property. Each time they tried to drill a hole into her neighbour's soil, the drill bit would snap as it was repelled by the hard, compacted ground. But when they drilled into the soil on Clara's side of the fence, the drill permeated her friable, moist, crumbly soil with ease.

Clara's farm had been just like the neighbours' when she and her husband, Alan, arrived seven years earlier — namely, overgrazed and eroded. But they worked hard to learn how to rebuild the humus in the soil, promoting microbial and fungal life, encouraging diverse and deep-rooting plant communities, planting trees and shrubs, and judiciously rotationally cell-grazing their slow-growing Black Angus cattle. Gradually they restored the property to the point where the pastures are thick with life and the soil is able to remain vibrant, despite increasingly frequent and long dry spells. (According to her neighbour, it also rains more on Clara's property, which is why, apparently, the grass is greener on her side of the fence.)

As Rob Lennon, an organic Wagyu beef farmer with whom we've worked for the past 10 years, said to us recently: 'The climate has changed and there are more extended dry periods. When the rain comes, it's heavier, and it's falling in winter and summer when it's not the best time for pasture to grow. Pasture is two-thirds what it was 20 years ago; it's not my right to continually graze it.'

Which brings us to beef.

The miracle of the ruminant

Like all ruminants, every day cows wake up and perform an amazing magic trick by transforming fibrous plant material (cellulose) into energy and protein, and providing manure and urine back to the soil to promote growth. It's astonishing to look at fully mature cattle and understand that these majestic creatures are the synthesis and distillation of simple pasture and forage. For millennia, all over the world, grasslands and herds of ruminants have evolved to thrive in a mutually beneficial, symbiotic relationship. The animals move across the grasslands, grazing for short, intense periods, fertilising the soil, mulching in organic matter with their hooves and grazing the grasses in such a way as to stimulate regrowth. Then they move on to leave the land to rest and the next act follows — the insects, birds and small creatures that benefit from the surface disruption and break down the manure and organic matter, which feeds the soil and promotes new life above and below the surface.

It was beef farmer Rob Lennon who taught us to see the beauty in cow manure, and gave us a powerful lesson in the connection between good beef and

'I'm a microbe farmer. I don't grow beef, I grow soil.'

Rob Lennon, Gundooee Organics Wagyu farmer

good soil. Standing in the middle of a paddock at his Gundooee Organics farm, Rob, who looks a bit like an antipodean Bob Dylan, picked up a cow pat and waved it excitedly in the air. Cattle manure, he explained, is an excellent marker of the digestive health of the cow — and, by extension, the health of the pasture, water and soil. Healthy soils produce healthy plants which, combined with clean water, produce healthy cow gut biota. This allows the cow to break down the forage, absorb the nutrients and minerals, and produce fine, beautifully fermented cow pats — not too dry, not too wet — which break down easily with the help of insects such as dung beetles, returning beneficial organic matter to the soil. Cows are like huge, mobile fermentation vats, extracting what they need and depositing the rest on the pasture in the form of fertiliser. But poor-quality water and soils result in compromised gut biota that inhibit fermentation and produce rough, coarse cow pats that are slow to break down. Despite three years of what some call the worst drought in living memory — punctuated by a savage bushfire that stripped his farm of pasture — Rob's soil remains crumbly and airy, able to soak up water and allow plant roots to permeate. Rob has worked hard over the past 20 years to repair and regenerate his farm and, in our humble opinion, he also produces some of the best beef in Australia. He is justifiably proud of his fine cow pats.

Healthy vegetation can only occur when the soil communities are healthy. When the stocking levels are too high for the specific location or season, the whole system suffers. But if the farmer allows close observation of the ecosystem to help determine stocking levels and they are moved regularly, then the whole system can benefit. The best farmers, like the conductor of a symphony, know how to orchestrate this movement to the advantage of the entire system in which the cows, for example, comprise merely the horn section. Once you see things this way, there's no going back. The world is revealed as a network of natural systems, and none of its moving parts can be improved or sustained unless the whole is considered in concert.

As Rob Lennon says, 'I'm a microbe farmer. I don't grow beef, I grow soil.'

If beef is the concentrated essence of the goodness that is inherent in healthy, vibrant soil, it's not hard to extrapolate that idea and see how it affects all of us, carnivore, vegetarian or vegan. Whether it's a cow or a carrot, if you're eating

Let's talk

something that depended on and absorbed the qualities of the soil on or in which it lived, then by extension you are also eating that soil.

By contrast, the conventional or intensive production of beef finished on grain in feedlots provides a really disturbing and puzzling logic.

In a feedlot, cattle are kept in pens and fed grain to fatten for market. However, as ruminants that have evolved to eat grasses, the grain-only diet initially produces a toxic digestive reaction that makes cattle sick until their systems adjust. Then, just like us when we eat a lot of grain and don't do any exercise, cattle quickly put on weight, thereby speeding up the process from feedlot to market. This process is often assisted by growth hormones that are given to cattle just before they enter the feedlot. (Not that you or your butcher are likely to know if the beef they're buying or selling has been administered growth hormones or not. When an animal is booked in for slaughter, the producer is required to fill out a detailed disclosure form that covers a range of questions including the administration of growth hormones. This form is entered into a database that allows for carcass traceability. However, that information doesn't accompany the carcass on its journey from the abattoir to your table, and the database isn't readily accessible to retail butchers like us. So, once the animal is slaughtered and the carcass is broken up into different parts and these parts are dispatched to different wholesalers and then onto multiple retailers, it's difficult to find out much at all about the animal you're selling or eating.) In the feedlot, cattle stand in their manure, which piles up, creating a waste problem that doesn't exist when cattle are rotated regularly from paddock to paddock to graze and fertilise the pastures.

So, in the intensive system, first we clear forests to grow crops peppered with chemicals designed to accelerate production. Then we transport the grain from these crops huge distances, and feed the grain to a herbivore that sickens initially because it isn't designed to eat grain. Then we harvest the animals, often transporting the meat huge distances, and we sell it in a market that doesn't value environmental management, animal welfare, species diversity, community welfare or the nutritional profile of the meat. At the same time, some 10 per cent of the omnivorous, grain-eating humans in the world are undernourished and one in four children are stunted from malnutrition.

The hair-raising calculations of what inputs are needed to produce a kilogram of meat and the resulting carbon footprint of cattle — which are often bandied about as unassailable proof that livestock agriculture is the root of all evil — are based on this deeply flawed, intensive production system.

But, as regenerative farmers all over the world are demonstrating, it doesn't have to be this way. The alternative is a much more benign agricultural system that includes livestock and improves fertility and capacity for all living things. But it will require a shift in attitude and behaviour — and we all have a role to play here. We are complicit if we choose to remain ignorant and buy food that is produced in unsustainable systems that support poor land management and damage our natural resources. Such food may be cheap now, but we and our children will pay the full price later as the costs of land mismanagement fall due. There's no doubt that it requires commitment to resist the lure of cheap meat and the idea that meat should be the mainstay of every meal. Despite the fact that healthier animals produce more nutritionally complete meat, which means you need to eat less of it to feel satiated, it's true that regeneratively produced meat is often more expensive. But where there's a will, there's a way. There are plenty of recipe suggestions in this book for cooking the cheaper cuts. Also, as we've advocated for years, we should all be eating a little less meat and expanding our diets to include greater balance and a wider variety of seasonal plants.

There are health implications too, because, not surprisingly, there's a direct correlation between microbial vitality in the soil and microbial vitality in the human gut. Everything is connected.

A message of hope

Soil health, the foundation for thriving ecosystems, can be restored. It takes time, patience and commitment, but it's possible. Across the world, regenerative farmers are choosing to manage land for the long term instead of for short-term gain, ecosystems are being transformed, and the precious diversity that guarantees capacity is returning. As the farmers we work with are demonstrating, the message of hope is that all of this can be achieved within a remarkably short space of time — less than a generation.

Many of the farmers we know have had 'Eureka!' moments, causing them to screech to a halt on the conventional road and veer sharply off track in pursuit of a much more nuanced, sensitive and responsive approach. They are clever, patient,

'Resilient, diverse, thriving ecosystems produce the most wonderful produce.'

fastidious, passionate and determined, and their idea of 'long term' is decades and centuries. They not only feed us, but take it upon themselves to repair, improve and revitalise the land to ensure continued fertility and productivity.

While they don't often turn out the huge volumes that intensive feed-lot or shed-based farms produce, regenerative farmers seem to be able to build ever-increasing capacity on their farms. Taking their cue from the soil, their mantra is 'Never bare the earth', which means moving animals regularly to avoid overgrazing and to allow for pasture and soil regeneration. It means constantly adjusting the number of animals on the farm to match the season, and only ever stocking the number of animals that the farm can sustain without overloading the system. It means always ensuring that pastures include a diverse mix of mutually beneficial native and exotic plants. It means reintroducing or protecting trees that act as huge carbon and water sponges and provide crucial habitat for a wide range of animals — all of which contribute, in some way, to the overall resilience of the system. It means seeking holistic solutions to land and animal management that don't undermine the network of natural relationships, and respecting and nurturing every element that contributes to the health of the farm community. It means being as proud of the diversity of plants in their paddocks as they are of the animals that graze upon them.

We are not farmers, but we do know quite a lot about really good-quality produce. What we've observed from working with some visionary farmers over the past 14 years is that, while they're busy saving our soil, farmers who are building inherently resilient, diverse, thriving ecosystems also produce the most impressive, nutritious, wonderful produce. Hands down.

The loam and the fishes

A wonderful example of this holistic approach is the story of the Southern Pygmy Perch at Moorlands Biodynamic Farm.

Vince Heffernan is rare among Australian farmers for several reasons. He's the sixth generation of his family to manage Moorlands, 3000 acres on the Lachlan River, near Dalton, an hour or so out of Canberra. That's a blink of an eye compared to the millennia of Indigenous Australian land management, but a long time in European settler history. However, while Vince continues the family business of raising livestock on his gently undulating pastures, every other aspect of his farm management is dramatically different from his forebears.

Instead of automatically prioritising human goals above all else and placing himself unassailably at the centre of his universe, Vince takes an 'ecocentric' rather than 'egocentric' approach to managing his land. Vince's requirement to earn an income from his land is equal in importance to the needs of all the other plants and animals. As custodian of his land, it is his obligation to nurture the long-term health of the entire community of creatures within the farm. So, in addition to growing the excellent, award-winning Texel lambs that we've been buying seasonally for 10 years, Vince and Janet Heffernan, a horticulturalist, have spent two decades regenerating their Demeter-certified biodynamic farm in an effort to restore the necessary diversity required to create capacity and health all round. The results are inspiring.

During our visits over the past 10 years in different seasons and conditions, we've observed a profoundly different approach at work on other farms in the area: overgrazed paddocks that looked like stubbled moonscapes of compacted, bare earth interrupted by jagged erosion canyons, with few trees or shrubs, and dotted with hollow-flanked cattle searching for food. The local Lachlan River course is denuded of plants, collapsing in on itself and choking with silt.

By comparison, at Moorlands, the cardinal regenerative rule of never baring the earth dictates a judicious grazing program that sees sheep constantly rotated through pastures. Years of carefully considered native tree and shrub plantings across the property aid water retention, improve organic matter and provide habitats that have attracted the return of birds and other creatures that haven't been seen in the area for many years. The Heffernans' stretch of Lachlan River frontage is dense with reintroduced endemic plants, and the regular deep pools that would once have provided critical habitats for diverse aquatic creatures and encouraged healthy water flow are forming again in the river course.

But the most striking expression of the 'ecocentric' management practice at this sixth-generation sheep farm is the fish sanctuary. The sanctuary is a secluded dam, fringed with local aquatic plants, propagated and carefully transplanted, and is dedicated to the rehabilitation of the critically endangered Southern Pygmy Perch, whose habitat is disappearing because of the damage caused by agricultural mismanagement of the Lachlan River catchment.

Many would view the Heffernans' decision to spend a lot of money and time building a dam, fencing it off, planting it out with appropriate species and managing it as a wildlife reserve for an endangered local fish as sheer lunacy — particularly because there's no expectation of earning a return from it, beyond the satisfaction of helping to save a species and contributing to a diverse ecosystem of communities.

We think it's pretty remarkable.

It takes years of hard work, devotion and skill to restore and rejuvenate complex communities of creatures on a farm — and, at the same time, deliver an award-winning meat product year after year.

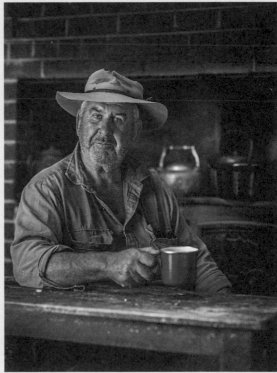

Community farmers like the Heffernans and others who take a similar approach should be rewarded with our loyalty and support for the work they're doing to nurture the land on our collective behalf. After all, it's farmers like these who are, literally, saving the earth for all of us.

Top: *One of the fish sanctuaries established by lamb farmers the Heffernans at Moorlands.*
Above right: *Vince Heffernan, biodynamic lamb farmer and fish protector.*

Never bare the earth

3.
It takes all sorts

The importance of diversity

If we understand that the ground on which we walk is simply the surface of a complex, pulsing subterranean world of communities of cooperating species, then we can understand that what lives above the ground must be equally rich, complex and diverse.

Let's talk

N o matter how hard we try to banish diversity and impose strict monocultures, the knotty, escalating mess of interventions required to repress nature's urge towards diversity is proof that nature won't take no for an answer.

We push it down in one corner and it pops up in another. We rush over with our arsenal of interventions and blast the latest infraction to bits but, out of the corner of our eye, we see it rise up again elsewhere.

Antibiotic resistance is a case in point. For years, livestock producers have routinely administered prophylactic antibiotics to intensively raised livestock to prevent the inevitable outbreaks of disease that occur when you jam a lot of animals together in a small area for extended periods. It turned out that the antibiotics also accelerated growth, which was an added bonus. But over the past 15 years, there have been increasing indications that this practice may turn out to be a very unwise squandering of a precious tool for managing human diseases. As the scale and spread of intensive livestock farming escalates across the world, the levels of residual antibiotics now in the food chain has actually rendered some antibiotics largely ineffective for human treatment. Even more disturbingly, there is evidence now that species-specific diseases have evolved to withstand antibiotics — and presented with the opportunities generated by unnatural, intensive livestock production, they are starting to jump species (so-called 'zoonotic' infections). The idea that we can contain nature is simply wishful thinking.

When we started our butchery adventure, we were dimly aware of these wider concerns, but very clear about the importance of diversity. Grant was mystified by the narrow offering available in the world of meat. There was 'lamb' and 'beef' and 'pork' and 'chicken', but almost no differentiation by breed, or location or production method — no way to distinguish between one offering and another. Compared to the rich diversity in the world of wine, this seemed a bizarre anomaly. Why were grapes and the process of making them into wine valued so differently from the business of growing an animal and turning it into food? Where were all the different breeds, and why wasn't anyone offering them? The more we learned about breeds, the more the world of meat opened up into a fascinating kaleidoscope of textures, shapes and flavours.

We started to appreciate the importance of a broad genetic palette: different breeds suit different landscapes, different breeds produce different carcasses, different breeds provide a different table product, and so on.

Faster, bigger, cheaper

We also started to understand that, with a few exceptions, industrialised meat production is a monochromatic landscape featuring a small handful of breeds that have been honed for docility, maximum meat yield and fast growth. Without consumers even realising it, the many benefits of slower-growing animals have been traded off in favour of a handful of breeds that meet our collective addiction to the commercial imperative of faster, bigger, cheaper. Wherever you go, these breeds dominate, offering a bland but consistent and predictable consumer experience, and constraining the all-important need for genetic diversity. Of course, there's nothing inherently wrong with consistency and predictability. But if the short-term realisation of these attributes comes at the cost of long-term, sustainable health, resilience and flavour, then you'd have to wonder about the real value of the system and who is really benefitting from it.

In this system, sheep are often the nervy Merino cross — a dual-purpose by-product of the wool industry. Good, but not the first breed that you'd choose if you were looking for outstanding eating qualities. Cattle are increasingly big, black, fast-growing, American-style Angus that are finished on grain in feedlots and slaughtered at the age of 14–18 months, before any real flavour profile develops. Pigs are fast-growing, white-haired breeds such as Landrace, with long, lean bodies bred to yield more of the belly and loins that sell so well, and less of the fat that we've been taught to avoid over the past few decades.

Meat chickens are uniformly the white Cobb or Ross breed — what the industry calls a 'standard white broiler', with a disproportionately large breast and remarkably fast-growing genetics: one of these birds raised in a shed can go from 5 grams when hatched to 2.2 kilograms in 35 days. That's a super-efficient, short-term protein and money machine, never mind the long-term implications. Eggs come from prolific, brown, hybrid Hyline or ISA Brown chickens that have been bred to energetically pump out even, brown eggs

'We have a collective addiction to the commercial imperative of faster, bigger, cheaper.'

their production declines, at which point, in the intensive system, they are sent off for pet food, or euthanised and composted. (Even pasture-based egg farmers who are happy to accommodate brief seasonal breaks in laying find that the economics of egg production mean that, when a chicken's output drops off and they're considered 'spent', they need to either be composted and recycled back into the farm or re-homed. At Extraordinary Pork, a pasture-based pig farm in New South Wales, spent laying hens from Farmer Brown, a pastured egg farm nearby, range across the paddocks with the heritage Berkshire pigs, fertilising the pastures and keeping the insect populations in balance. They are excellent pasture workers, and the intermittent eggs they lay are a welcome bonus for their owners and the pigs.)

The narrow focus on breeds selected exclusively for speed to market is particularly stark in the conventional dairy industry. Most of the commercial milk supply comes from black and white Holstein cows that have been narrowly bred with a ferocious commitment to increased production. Since 1950, the output per cow in the United States, for example, has risen five-fold, while in a similar period, industry consolidation has reduced the number of dairies by half. In commercial terms, this is a bonanza, and there's no doubt that these 'super cows' are incredibly efficient milk machines: fewer cows, more milk, cheaper! But this genetic escalation in production capacity comes at a cost to the overall health of the cows, as well as a reduction in the quality and nutritional value of our dairy produce, and it also gives rise to the escalating problem of what to do with the male calves. The market price for 5-day-old male calves doesn't justify the cost of freight and slaughter, but consumer appetite for veal has declined, so few farmers find it economical to grow male calves out. Increasingly, the economic and welfare costs of running a small dairy outweigh the returns, and the system seems to make everyone except the supermarkets and the end consumer pretty miserable.

But it doesn't have to be this way. The bucolic Burraduc Buffalo Farm is a model of 'ecocentric' over 'egocentric' farming, in which biodiversity and the collective health of all the creatures in the food chain, including predators, is prioritised.

Learning to share buffalo milk and live with dingoes

A buffalo dairy farm that challenges convention and insists on the right of all creatures to co-exist in the landscape.

At Burraduc, a regeneratively managed, coastal buffalo dairy farm in the Myall Lakes district of New South Wales, Elena and Andrei Swegen chose a dairy production model based on the radically different principle of sharing milk with their buffalo calves. The convention in the intensive dairy model dictates that the new-born calf stays with the cow long enough to receive the colostrum that is crucial for providing antibodies and healthy gut bacteria, after which the two are separated so that the cow can give all her milk to the farmer. By contrast, at Burraduc, the buffalo calves aren't weaned until they are 5–6 months old. Each morning, the buffalo cows walk from the paddock through the on-farm dairy gate to be milked, after which they spend the day with their calves, feeding and ranging together across the paddocks. In the evening, they wander back to the dairy with the calves in tow and allow their babies to be separated and placed into a separate pen together while the cows return to spend the night in the paddocks. In the morning, the cows turn up again for milking and, after giving the farmer a share of their milk, they are reunited with their calves and wander the farm for the rest of the day. Male calves grow alongside their sisters until they begin to display sexual behaviour at around six to seven months, at which point they are sent off to the abattoir and become buffalo veal, which is consumed on the farm and sold to Burraduc customers.

It's absolutely true that this system of sharing milk results in lower volumes of dairy products for sale and, if you're producing less volume, then the market value of what you do sell must be high for the business to survive. Which, as always, brings us back to the question of how any one of us measures value — simply by price? Or should we be incorporating environmental, human and animal welfare impact and the nutritional value of a product into the shelf price?

However you choose to answer those questions, at Burraduc, the sharing model produces undeniably successful outcomes. The pastures are abundant, the calves are well-fed and healthy, the buffalo cows are content and living as naturally as possible, their milk is a rich expression of all the genetic and environmental goodness available on the farm and, in Elena's skilful hands, it becomes award-winning cheese, passing all those minerals and vitamins — the concentrated health and vitality of the farm — to us.

Originally from Moscow, the Swegens are scientists who bred and farmed animals in various parts of Australia before finding the perfect location to grow their Riverine buffalo on the lush, sub-tropical, mid-northern coast of New South Wales. It's an idyllic landscape abutting a national park and, even in winter and during drought, the paddocks are covered with lush grasses dotted with grand buffalo cows and limpid-eyed, wet-nosed calves.

*At Burraduc, Central
Asian Shepherd Dogs
protect the buffalo calves
and other domestic
animals and discourage
feral cats, foxes and
local dingoes.*

Let's talk

'The Swegens believe in the importance of species diversity.'

In addition to running a radically different dairy model, the Swegens believe in the importance of species diversity and the right of all creatures to co-exist in the landscape.

Every ecosystem has its predator–prey and, when the system is in balance, each one of these creatures plays an important role in maintaining sustainable populations and preserving the overall health of the system. In Australia, the peak animal predator is the dingo, which for millennia has co-evolved with the landscape and other animals to keep the ecosystem in balance. But dingoes are hunters, so offer them a fenced paddock full of unprotected sheep with no instinctive capacity to protect themselves and the dingoes will, of course, do what comes naturally, much to the ire and distress of the sheep farmers. In response, farmers run aggressive campaigns, poisoning and shooting the dingoes in an attempt to eradicate them.

But, in the face of the increasing evidence that Australia's native flora and fauna are in deep trouble from the combined impact of introduced species and loss of habitat from conventional agricultural practices, the Swegens argue for a more tolerant and nuanced response. Not only do dingoes have a right to inhabit the landscape as they did for thousands of years prior to the arrival of sheep farmers, but they also have a critical role to play in maintaining ecosystem balance. Additionally, they keep destructive introduced species like foxes, rabbits and feral cats in check. Feral cats, in particular, are much more savage hunters than dingoes and without a predator (like the dingo) to keep them in check, have played a huge part in wiping out many species of small marsupials and native birds.

At Burraduc, the Swegens refuse to shoot or poison dingoes or any other wild animals. Instead, they use Central Asian Shepherd Dogs to keep dingoes at bay and protect their domesticated animals, which include buffalo calves, a few sheep and chickens. As a result, although the farm borders the national park in which the dingoes live, and their neighbours report problems with wild dogs, the Swegens very rarely see dingoes. In addition, there are no destructive rabbits colonising and digging up the farm, and the kangaroos that compete with grazing livestock for available fodder in times of drought give the farm a wide berth.

Of course, it's more work to choose to run a dairy farm this way. Buffalo are wilder than dairy cows and require careful husbandry, sharing the milk means more movement and handling of animals, and the livestock guardian dogs are another species to manage. But when the system sings, as it does at Burraduc, the overall benefits of this benign approach that fosters and embraces diversity ripple all the way from the farm to us, concentrated in each nutritious mouthful of yoghurt or buffalo cheese.

Opposite top: Elena Swegen with recently weaned calves — Riverine buffalo are wilder and less docile than domesticated cattle.
Opposite bottom: After morning milking, the cows are reunited with their calves to spend the day together wandering the pastures.

The natural urge towards diversity

The loss of species diversity in contemporary agriculture isn't limited to livestock. The varieties of plant foods grown for human and animal consumption has narrowed dramatically since industrialisation and the advent of intensive agricultural practices.

As the United Nations' Food and Agriculture Organisation reported in February 2019: 'Of some 6000 plant species cultivated for food, fewer than 200 contribute substantially to global food output, and only nine account for 66 per cent of total crop production.'

Modern plant breeding and selection is all about logistics, shelf life and unhealthy ideas of perfection, rather than seasonality, flavour, nutrition and the role plants play in ensuring the health of complex ecosystems.

Of course, you could argue that this exclusive focus on breeds and systems that produce the greatest volumes isn't entirely Machiavellian. By raising animals in sheds or feedlots, for example, you're confining production to a limited area and, by selecting for specific genetic traits to get more yield from each animal or plant, you're making the best use of resources. You're getting more product, faster — and the volumes mean it's cheaper for the consumer. That's all got to be good, right? If only it were that simple.

Aside from the fact that this intensive production regime largely disregards the experience of animals and relegates them to slave status where their only function is to produce food for us, the gains in production yield are being made at the expense of diversity and ecosystem balance, which is not good for our long-term health and prosperity. The entrancing idea that we can pluck out any one species and hothouse it for our specific needs runs contrary to the laws of nature, which doggedly insist that the only viable, healthy systems are those comprising a rich network of diverse species.

The natural urge towards diversity is undeniable. If you look at the unkempt verges running along the sides of country roads or any garden that's left to its own devices, you'll see this at work. Different species appear, jostling together, vigorously collaborating and competing, and collectively creating a dynamic, networked ecosystem that together makes everything healthier and stronger — the sum is greater than the parts.

All living creatures cluster together in like communities, whether we're microbes or humans, but all of us are also co-dependent for our health and wellbeing on all the millions of other creatures with which we interact every day. You only have to remember that your skin plays host to about 1000 different species of bacteria, fungi, viruses and mites to realise that there are critical, mutually beneficial interactions between life forms occurring everywhere, all the time. Everything we know about nature and evolution tells us that diversity produces capacity, and is critical to sustainable resilience and fertility. As soon as you narrow the palette too far, things start to go wrong, which is why human societies all over the world have always incorporated cultural rules that prevent in-breeding, maintain genetic diversity and keep our species evolving: stasis is the enemy of life. The battle for available resources determines the populations, variety and balance of different species within an ecosystem. The capacity to be flexible, to adapt and evolve — to diversify — is critical to survival.

But, as the spectacularly successful, dominant predator on earth, we humans increasingly seem to think that the resources on hand are infinite, that we've largely mastered nature, and that *we'll* decide where, when and how we have our diversity, thanks very much.

Curiously, while our insatiable appetite for growth is actually crippling natural diversity at every turn, the notion of 'diversity' has become more and more popular and is increasingly understood as central to human cultural resilience and creativity. No company or organisation with a public profile would be seen dead these days without a diversity employment policy to trumpet about.

On the other hand, when it comes to agriculture and what we feed ourselves, we're perfectly happy to drop diversity like a hot (Sebago) potato in favour of intensive monocultures that offer a narrowing long-term palette but huge short-term gains. Of course, the attraction of intensifying and concentrating production to gain huge advantages in speed and scale is overwhelmingly compelling, and it's obvious why monocultural agricultural systems dominate the landscape and the aisles of our supermarkets. For the consumer, it's all about convenience. For the producers, it's about efficiency and scale. Grow one thing, as much as possible, as fast as possible, distribute to as many people as possible, pocket the profit. Repeat. It's easy to see the appeal. But in the long term, this approach is an unsustainable hiding to nothing.

Land degradation — from excessive clearing, cultivation and grazing, and the damage caused by chemical inputs — has reduced the productivity of 23 per cent of the global land surface; each year, up to US$577 billion worth of global crops are at risk from pollinator loss, and 1 million of the 8 million animal and plant species in the world today are under threat of extinction. In May 2019, the United Nations' Intergovernmental Science-Policy Platform on Biodiversity and Ecosystem Services released the most comprehensive biodiversity report to date, which paints a sphincter-clenching picture of the current condition of the natural world and what will happen if we don't change our behaviour — immediately and everywhere. Riddled with chilling statistics, the overriding message is that we urgently need to understand the connection between the damage our growth model is doing to the natural world, and to our own long-term survival.

We are, literally, eating the hand that feeds us.

Taking the long view

In our business, we're very fortunate to work with the growing number of producers who are farming in a way that actively contributes to the long-term health, resilience, biodiversity and fertility of the land, and the communities it supports. Regenerative farming prioritises balance over yield and values nature's superior ability to self-organise in pursuit of fertility. The farmer's job is to find a way to meet their needs without compromising the dynamic interaction between every creature in the ecosystem. In fact, whatever it is that the farmer is growing — plants or animals — the process must contribute to the overall health and diversity rather than compromise or deplete the system. In recent years, we've seen a welcome increase in the consumer appetite for diversity in crops and livestock, enabling willing farmers to be more adventurous and explore different breeds and strains. Over the years we've welcomed dozens of different breeds of animals into our butchery, some of which are critically endangered and provide a powerful link to our agricultural past. As counter-intuitive as it might sound, if we don't keep eating these rare breeds, they won't survive because no one will grow them.

We've met all sorts of breeders and chicken fanciers and passionate fourth-generation farmers looking for breeds to help them tread more lightly on the earth and farm in a different way to their forebears — feeding the land that feeds us. We became obsessed with the glorious aesthetics of different breeds of pigs and chickens and fantasised about smuggling them into our suburban backyard in Sydney. (We did have some success hosting Brian and Sheila, a devastatingly beautiful pair of heritage-breed Belgian Campine chickens. But, not long after he arrived in our Marrickville garden, young Brian discovered his voice. Despite his firm belief that he was the Pavarotti of the chicken world, Brian's proud and earnest crowing, which he started practising at 3 a.m. each morning, was a uniquely horrible, blood-curdling

'If we don't keep eating these rare breeds, they won't survive.'

scream that sounded like a woman being murdered. After an outcry from the neighbours, we were compelled to pack him off to the country where we sadly later learned that not-so-fantastic Mr Fox got the better of him. Sheila remained, ruling the remaining Orpington Splash and Belgian Wyandotte chooks with her more moderate shriek, delivered during regular working hours, for the next decade.)

Every piece of meat we sell is identified by breed, and there is a gorgeous spectrum of diversity across the different farms. Some of the cattle include Red Angus, Galloway and Belted Galloway, Dexter, Wagyu, Hereford, Speckle Park and South Devon. Sheep include Southdown, Black and White Suffolk, Hampshire Down, Dorper, Texel, Australian White, Wiltshire Horn and Wiltipoll. Pigs include Berkshire, English Large Black, English Large White, Duroc, Tamworth and Wessex Saddleback. Among the meat chickens are Transylvanian Naked Necks, Indian Game, Plymouth Rock, Light Sussex and Aussie Game, while the ducks include Aylesbury, Pekin and Muscovy.

The farmers we work with are intent on either differentiating by brand, or value-adding as a way of thriving in a contracting industry.

Like all farmers, regenerative livestock farmers select the breeds they grow with great care, considering every facet of production from meat quality to genetic vitality and the fit with their particular production system. But, because the overall objectives and goals differ from those of conventional or intensive farmers, the end products are also very different.

If you're a farmer wanting to build a thriving ecosystem and produce the best-quality table produce from free-ranging animals raised outside on pasture, then you're looking for a very particular set of genetics that may not have much in common with those favoured by the intensive industry. White-skinned pigs, for example, are more vulnerable to sunburn and skin cancers so, if you're raising them outside in a country like Australia, you'd better be sure they've got plenty of shade and shelter. Instead, you might consider old-breed, black or multi-hued pigs that are hardy and instinctively know how to thrive outside in the elements, developing a layer of protective, delicious fat and providing flavoursome meat. On the other hand, if the meat is 'too' fatty, then consumers who have been encouraged over the past 30 years to view animal fats with deep suspicion might arc up and refuse to buy.

More mature, slower-growing animals generally offer the best texture and the deepest flavour. The difference between yearling beef (12–18 months) and 2–3-year-old pasture-raised beef, for example, is incomparable, and a growing number of consumers are cottoning on and seeking out more mature, better-quality, ethically raised meat. However, animals fattened in feedlots grow faster than those living their entire lives grazing freely on pasture. So despite the benefits that come with maturity and slow growth, every farm is a business, and the longer an animal is on pasture and the longer it takes to reach a marketable size, the more it costs. In a marketplace that prioritises speed and volume, it can be hard for a farmer or a butcher to earn a price that rewards the cost, time and work involved in producing a superior product with a beneficial environmental footprint.

When we first started our pursuit of different breeds of livestock, we found a small but growing number of farmers who were pasture-raising heritage meat breeds for commercial sale. It wasn't long before we were able to offer our customers half a dozen different sheep and cattle breeds, and a smaller number of heritage pig breeds. But we were stymied when it came to chicken. It took six years of searching high and low to find an option to the omnipresent white broiler bird — and another couple of years before it became a viable commercial product.

Born to be bland: the broiler chicken industry

Unless you've hunted down a heritage breed, every time you eat chicken, the chances are you are eating a white Cobb or Ross breed, which are so similar as to be interchangeable. They are the 'standard white broiler' that has been fine-tuned over the past 50 years to provide an irresistibly efficient meat bird that satisfies all the material requirements of our current market system. A bird that's been engineered to grow muscle before bone, and produces a high meat yield — mostly breast — very fast. A chicken living inside a temperature-controlled, aritficially lit shed with all its food and water laid on doesn't need to spend energy learning to negotiate the elements while keeping an eye out for predators, foraging for food or growing powerful legs and a strong skeleton to support itself. Instead, safe and sedentary inside the asylum, with nothing else to do, the chicken tucks in and puts on weight, very quickly.

It's hard to see how even a flock animal could enjoy living cheek by jowl with hundreds of other birds without enough room to spread its wings, or do the things that chickens do when they're free to roam around outside. Putting aside the question of whether this is a humane or fair way to treat a fellow animal, raising chickens in sheds appears to be a super-efficient way to convert a relatively small resource expenditure into a hugely popular source of protein. Except, of course, there's always a price when you cut corners to speed something up. In the case of intensively raised chickens (and pigs), there's a cascading avalanche of issues including safe waste disposal that doesn't pollute the natural environment, prophylactic antibiotic use to counteract the constant threat of disease and the drastic narrowing of the gene pool. Not surprisingly, intensively raised white broiler chicken meat is a singularly bland, inoffensive product that requires a lot of dressing up to achieve genuine flavour. A very limited life results in a very limited product.

The riotous success of the intensive white broiler chicken industry has dramatically reduced both the cost of chicken and our expectation of what it should taste like. What has increased, however, is how *often* we expect to eat it, and our perplexing willingness to turn a blind eye to the way this meat is produced.

Over the years, during our search for the elusive option to the white broiler chicken, we've worked with farmers who are successfully pasture-raising these Cobb or Ross broiler birds. Given the opportunity, the birds' nascent instincts start to come to the fore. They graze and scratch and sunbake and dust-bathe and their growth rates slow as they spend energy dealing with the Great Outdoors. Also, while they're pottering around outside on pasture, they're providing fertiliser, gently disturbing the soil surface and assisting plant regrowth, eating plants and insects, and fulfilling their role as predators in the ecological food chain. However, while the pastured method is vastly preferable from every perspective, the Cobb or Ross broiler is constrained by its super-fast growing genetics, and becomes less active as it gains weight.

Australian meat chicken production is an unnatural monoculture and it took us eight years to find a commercial meat chicken breed other than the ubiquitous standard white broiler. But in 2014, a shaft of light pierced the avian gloom and we discovered Michael and Kathryn Sommerlad and their heritage chicken breeding project.

A chicken revolution

Meet the Sommerlad chicken, a unique composite bird that includes up to seven different breeds in its genetic makeup.

Slower-growing, athletic and selectively bred over 15 years to thrive outside in the Australian climate, Sommerlad chickens happily manage the full spectrum of extreme summer heat and mid-winter cold with resilient equanimity.

Unlike the white broiler chickens that struggle to remain agile after 8 weeks of age, let alone cross the road, Sommerlad birds are a riot of colour and are built to run, hunt and explore with long, strong legs and powerful feet. After hatching, the downy chicks spend 2–3 weeks in the brooder growing protective feathers, before spending the next 9–12 weeks outside on pasture.

By contrast, the majority of white broiler chickens are bred and hatched at facilities owned by the small handful of vertically integrated poultry producers that dominate the industry. The day-old chicks are then distributed to hundreds of farms where they grow, mostly in sheds, until they reach market weight. It's extremely rare for chicken farmers to breed and hatch their own birds.

Michael Sommerlad, the chicken expert and breeder responsible for the eponymous bird, was spurred into action by the experience of spending years in the meat-chicken industry managing 'standard broiler' birds with most of the 'chicken-ness' bred out of them. In the 1990s, the white broiler took over completely, and producers sold off all other strains of meat chickens to concentrate production on this single breed.

Concerned about the loss of genetics (and knowledge), Michael purchased some of the birds that were suddenly homeless and continued to breed and foster these strains. Convinced that Australians would embrace a better alternative if they experienced it, Michael and Kathryn Sommerlad set about producing a slow-growing, flavoursome table bird. As they write, the Sommerlad bird is:

> … specifically bred to thrive in free-range, pasture-rearing environments. Because of this careful breeding, our chickens have a range of higher-welfare characteristics. These include active foraging behaviour, heat-resistance, balanced body confirmation and strong legs, as well as good liveability with improved, natural resistance to diseases endemic to Australian poultry flocks.

Sommerlad chickens are also remarkably animated in ways you don't see in standard white broiler birds. Adam and Fiona Walmsley grew Sommerlads for us a few years ago at their beautiful Buena Vista Farm near Kiama in New South Wales, and Adam had some very funny footage of Sommerlad chicks jumping up and swinging on a loose loop of the water-dripper inside the brooder. One swings and then another jumps up and knocks the swinger off so it can have a go, before being knocked off by the next one who thinks it must be their turn now. They were only two weeks old, and not yet feathered enough to go out onto pasture, but already displaying the curiosity, personality and resourcefulness that allows them to thrive outside.

Farmer and breeder Kim Kiss and Roger the Magnificent, the elder statesman of the Sommerlad heritage breeding flock at Grassland Poultry.

Let's talk

As well as delivering a multi-award-winning table bird with darker, deeply flavoured meat, thicker skin and golden fat, there's the skill it takes to breed and cross multiple generations of different breeding flocks to maximise the most desirable qualities to produce birds that are, literally, made for Australian pastures. It's one thing to grow some heritage-breed chickens; it's another thing altogether to breed new strains of chickens that can be reproduced consistently and at some scale in pasture-based production.

Then there are the handful of carefully selected, family-run farms that are breeding and raising the birds according to specific Sommerlad guidelines. Each farm is unique, but all are united by a profound commitment to diversity, and all are passionate, skilful trailblazers in small-scale, regenerative farming. Whether you eat meat or not, in our humble opinion the whole country owes a debt of gratitude to the Sommerlads for their remarkable work in reintroducing critical genetic diversity to the meat chicken industry, and to the small group of farmers with the courage and imagination to embrace the Sommerlad bird.

The Sommerlad chickens we sell are from Grassland Poultry and are bred and raised by Kim and Bryan Kiss in New South Wales. The Kisses embraced regenerative farming about 20 years ago, and have been cell grazing their beef cattle and working to rebuild soil health for years. They had been pasture-raising white broiler chickens, rotating the chickens across the paddocks after their cattle, and using Italian Maremma sheepdogs to protect the birds. But when they heard about the Sommerlad project, they immediately set about joining the small group of accredited Sommerlad farmers. At the time of writing, the Kisses have just completed construction of a small, on-farm chicken abattoir. This is a remarkable and rare achievement for a small-scale, regenerative farm and will allow them to control the entire production cycle from breeding and hatching through to slaughter, packaging and dispatch.

Changing behaviour, rethinking our assumptions of market value and weaning ourselves off the unsustainable monocultural food production treadmill is difficult. It means choosing to become more informed and accepting responsibility for our role in deciding what gets produced — and resisting the guilty, narcotic lure of impossibly cheap products. Cheap now, devastatingly expensive later.

If you think of your own gut biome as an ecosystem comprising communities of diverse flora that require equally diverse and healthy inputs to thrive, you can see how the idea of a diverse diet rich in many different kinds of vegetables, fruits and animal proteins might also enrich your individual, overall health. You might conclude that the notion of meat as the main source of protein and the hero of every meal narrows your options, and this revelation might send you scampering off to explore the banquet of seasonal plant possibilities at your local farmers' market. As long as you're holding the growers of those fruits and vegetables to account and ensuring that you spend your hard-earned cash on food that's produced out of systems that are transparent, traceable and build long-term fertility, then that's a very good thing.

But don't forget, whether you eat animals or not, unless we all support the work of farmers who are actively working to build biodiversity by farming regeneratively and choosing to grow a diverse range of livestock breeds, then we may find that those breeds disappear — and the entire global ecosystem will be poorer for the loss.

Top left: *Sommerlad chick in the brooder, about 1 week old, at Grassland Poultry, NSW.*
Top right: *99 per cent of Australian chickens are white broiler chickens. Grassland Poultry is one of a handful of farms growing a variety of chicken breeds that provide a welcome splash of colour and genetic diversity.*
Bottom: *Three different expressions of Sommerlad genetics, Grassland Poultry, NSW.*

Michael Hicks at the door of his abattoir on Extraordinary Pork pastured-pig farm, NSW.

4.
Looking the animal in the eye

Understanding the slaughter process

While it's tempting to avert our gaze, we all bear responsibility for engaging honestly and compassionately with the realities of life and death.

As the famous self-described 'lunatic farmer', Joel Salatin, so eloquently puts it, 'It's how we honour and respect the least of these that creates an ethical framework around which we honour and respect the greatest of these.'

Joel's particular brand of lunacy insists that fertility *and* profitability can be increased while employing more people on a diverse range of productive enterprises, all on the one farm. Here, though, he is drawing our attention to what should be the humbling task of killing animals for food, and reminding us that it is serious work that requires both a clear head and a steady hand, but also an honourable intent. While maintaining a clear-eyed appreciation of the stark realities, this chapter attempts to unpick the industrial processes that bring meat to our table — starting with Grant's first visit to a farm. Here's his story.

Hold on tight!

When I was nine years old and in Year 5 at primary school, I was selected to take part in an exchange program where a few city kids spent a week in the country, staying with a host family and attending school with one of the family's children of the same age. The schools were selected for their remote location and tiny size, with none having more than two classrooms. The following week I would come back to the city with my new-found friend Robert, who would get to see what it was like to attend a big city primary school with several hundred students.

The family to whom I was assigned were dairy farmers in the south Gippsland region of southern Victoria, which is an area that is mostly cold, usually wet and, on the better soils at least, perfect for dairying. It was a small farm by today's standards — only about 95 hectares, with what I probably described in my subsequent school report as 'a lot of cows', but was actually somewhere around 180 milkers. The gruelling rhythm of twice-daily milking topped and tailed each day. The family also ran a handful of mature sheep on the side that they kept for their meat.

Left: *Alexandra Hicks herds a small group down the lane towards the on-farm abattoir at Extraordinary Pork, NSW. Read about this extra-ordinary farm on page 76.*

It was my first exposure to farm life, and while many eye-opening things occurred that week, one incident in particular really stayed with me. The morning milking had finished and there was just the clean-up to go. Robert's father was relaxed after getting the best part of the morning's work done, and was joking around with us boys. He encouraged me to ride one of the sheep that were penned near the milking yards. I wasn't at all sure whether I should really be doing this, considering I was at least as big, if not as heavy, as the sheep and it seemed a little unfair, but Robert's dad was insistent. Reluctantly, I straddled the sheep's back, but there was only the fleece to hold on to, and I remember thinking that if I held on too tightly I would hurt the sheep, like having your hair pulled. Needless to say that, with only a loose grip of its wool, when the alarmed animal took a huge leap forward, I fell off immediately, tumbling off its back and landing in the muck left over from the just-milked cows. Predictable and comical, the know-nothing city boy was undone.

I was still considering my miserable options when Robert's father suddenly grabbed one of the other sheep and flipped it onto its bottom with its back up against his legs. The sheep restrained as if about to be shorn, but instead of shears Robert's dad produced a knife, and holding the sheep's head up and to one side, quickly drew the blade across its exposed neck, leaving a brilliant ruby red line in its wake. With the next contraction of the sheep's heart, its life's blood spurted out towards me. Up until then I hadn't witnessed anything bigger than a fish dying. Something from the sea. Something fundamentally other. But here was a creature, certainly no smaller than me — and like me, a warm-blooded creature — about to breathe its last. It was both completely unexpected and totally shocking. But what made the experience indelible was when Robert's father looked up and, seeing me standing there covered in cow shit, shot me a big smile and said, 'I only had to do this because you've come to stay.'

Robert's dad probably didn't realise the impact that his throw-away line would have on me, but there was no doubt that dinner tasted … different

'Robert's father shot me a big smile and said, "I only had to do this because you've come to stay."'

after that. This was all my fault and I better enjoy it, except I didn't much. Of course, looking back on it now, it's likely that this demonstration of the visceral realities of farm life was a calculated ploy, a necessary part of my rural education, and Robert's father's way of saying, 'Welcome to the farm!'

But aside from the animals that are killed on a farm to feed the people who live there, the vast majority of meat that is sold in Australia for human consumption is derived from farmed animals that are killed in licensed abattoirs. Certainly, this is the case for all of the meat we sell in our butchery.

And we, along with the farmers who raised them and the customers who buy from us, are implicated in the deaths of literally thousands of creatures each year, from the tiny 6-week-old, 800-gram quail right through to the massive 6-year-old, 800-kilogram cow.

What follows is a discussion of what happens in these places, and the journey that is undertaken from the farm to the abattoir, and the abattoir to our cool room. If the temptation is to skip this chapter and jump straight to the recipe section, because learning how an animal became your dinner is just too confronting or gruesome, we implore you to bear with us, because Joel Salatin is right when he says that if slaughter isn't built on respect, it can only be seen as a brutal and wanton taking of life. And this respect must also extend to the people who do this work on our behalf. So while I now know that I wasn't solely responsible for the death of that sheep, I'm not completely off the hook either, because whenever we sit down to eat meat we are connected to that animal's life, and the life it gave up to feed us. And for those of us who believe that the exchange of the life of another being for the nourishment of a few is desirable, or even possible, then the light we shine on that process becomes vitally important.

This chapter attempts to look at the organised killing of terrestrial farmed animals for food in a clear-eyed manner. And perhaps I should say now what I wished Robert's father had said to me before the indignant sheep took off: 'Hold on tight!'

Animals to the slaughter: the importance of low-stress handling

Over an average year, we source from up to 15 different abattoirs, most located in our home state of New South Wales. Some of these abattoirs process many hundreds of animals in a single day — even many thousands in the case of one large-scale organic chicken abattoir — while three are tiny on-farm abattoirs, located on the farm that produces the animals that they slaughter. That's an important difference, as transport to the abattoir can be a very stressful event for the animals. And stress is to be avoided at all costs, both to ensure their death is as quick and painless as possible, thus fulfilling our obligations to the animals in our care, but also to maintain optimum meat quality. It is crucial that an animal has high levels of glycogen (a form of glucose that is stored mainly in the muscles and liver) in its system prior to slaughter.

The effects of lengthy transport and the unfamiliar environment of the abattoir with its foreign noises and smells, along with the presence of many other animals previously unknown to them, all add up to a potentially traumatic experience. For these animals we only have one chance to get it right.

The cumulative stress of these experiences will gallop through their available glycogen reserves, and if there is not enough of it, their meat will be tough, dark and dry. Following death, glucose in the blood converts to lactic acid, reducing the overall pH level in the muscle tissue. A final pH of 5.5 or 5.6 is critical for flavour, tenderness and the keeping quality of the meat. (Rob Lennon from Gundooee Organics specifically feeds his sale cattle a small ration of copra meal, a coconut by-product, to elevate their glycogen levels just before transport to the abattoir. In this way he tries to ensure that the carcasses that arrive at our shop a few days later are the best possible reflection of up to 4 years of careful husbandry from conception to slaughter.)

Undue stress at slaughter, especially in pigs and poultry, gives rise to the charmingly named condition known as Pale, Soft, Exudative meat (PSE meat), which accurately describes the unusable result and is associated with abnormally low pH levels.

The thoughtful farmer will do their utmost to ensure that all of the interactions they have with their stock, that the stock have with each other, and what and how they are fed and watered from birth to death, combine to produce an animal with the most trusting and calm disposition possible, and, crucially, that their animals are able to express most, if not all, of their instinctive behaviours — precisely because those conditions will allow the fullest possible expression of the genetic potential of the animals in their care. This is what we mean when we talk about quality meat; it is the coalescence of the qualities inherent in that animal that is brought to full realisation through considered management under the prevailing seasonal conditions.

A critical element of that individual animal's maximum possible expression is achieved through the practice of 'low-stress stock handling', which works *with* their natural responses and tendencies as much as possible, rather than *against* them. It is also a recognition of the individuality of that animal, and that its precise nutritional requirements, say, will be subtly different from the animal that is grazing quietly nearby.

Many of us will have grown up with film and television images of great mobs of cattle being herded with lots of people yelling, whips cracking and dogs barking, all overlaid with a swelling orchestral score that bespeaks human triumph over animals. While a well-trained, well-mannered dog or three can and do play a part in the modern practice of herding sheep, cattle, pigs and goats, the farmers we work with make every effort to keep the whole process decidedly undramatic. It should be quiet, simple and as predictable for animal and human as possible. (There are even farmers who are encouraging self-herding, eschewing fencing entirely, and moving mobs of sheep and cattle by using visual cues in the landscape that the animals have learned to associate with the presence of food and water.) By recognising the extraordinary — almost 360-degree — peripheral vision of a cow, for example, and by positioning yourself out of their flight zone, you can keep the animals' stress levels low while getting them to go where you want, without the use of force. Since all of the farmers we work with practise some form of rotational, time-managed grazing, frequent opportunities for calm animal–human interaction abound. And having people who transport your animals also being aware of these sensitivities extends the predictable management to which the animals have become accustomed.

Most of us have heard of the term 'bellwether', without realising its agricultural origins. In European rural uplands and highlands used for summer grazing, one sheep would be belled. Crucially, it was the lead sheep, which the rest of the flock would follow, that would wear the bell. From a shepherd's perspective it's simple: listen for the bell and you find your sheep, all of them. The same principle applies when you are trying to load animals onto a truck to transport them to the abattoir. For many animals this will be the first time they've used anything but their own feet to go anywhere, so getting them on the truck as calmly as possible is critical. Choose the leader and the rest are much more inclined to follow. Choose the straggler and nothing short of too-frequent use of electric prods and brandished lengths of poly-pipe will get the job done, with distressed and bruised animals and appreciable loss of valuable blood sugar (and saleable meat) the unacceptable results.

This is Extraordinary

This farm runs a rare system in which the pasture-raised pigs' entire life cycle occurs on the farm.

In 2012, Michael and Alexandra Hicks moved onto their property on the outskirts of Dubbo, NSW. It was a 140-hectare (350-acre) farm with a decades-long history of over-grazing by sheep and a general air of not-so-benign neglect, if the removal of four semi-trailer loads of rusting farm equipment and other 'assets' belonging to the previous owner was anything to go by. Alex had always wanted to raise pigs, and with the help of Michael's extensive agricultural training and experience, the Hicks decided this was the place to pursue their dream. But from the outset they decided it must be an enterprise that was good for the pigs, good for the land, and good for their quality of life. So, apart from changing the primary enterprise from sheep-meat and wool to pigs, and implementing systems designed for animal welfare and land improvement, they were also intent on establishing a farm that had the infrastructure to allow Michael to handle the bulk of the day-to-day operations by himself.

The characteristics of the local soil profile combined with decades of land mismanagement meant that rain, when it fell, tended to run off the surface, rather than soak into the soil. To address this, the Hicks employed a leading regenerative farm planner to carefully survey the cleared areas to determine the exact route of a new, gently sloping service road, which now allows access to most of the paddocks that their 120 grower pigs, boar and sows will rotate through over the year. The same cleverly contoured road also acts as a primary water collector, draining directly to the main dam which, together with a second dam set higher in the landscape, make the entire farm water secure, even deep in an unrelenting drought, in a region where most farmers are completely reliant on poor-quality bore water.

The Extraordinary Pork herd is dominated by Berkshire genetics, a large, slower-growing, mostly black-haired breed that is a common choice for outdoor-reared pigs in Australia. (Confusingly, it is sometimes marketed as Kurobuta, which is the Japanese name for a particular strain of this breed, and simply means 'black pig'.) Coupled with an infusion of mixed Duroc/Berkshire blood via their new boar, Bob Marley (so-called because of his calm temperament rather than his lifestyle choices), his progeny display a relaxed swagger along with robust conformation, the latter quality largely courtesy of the Duroc line.

The Hicks' animal management practice reflects their regeneratively minded ethos. It is a system designed to be both simple to operate and predictable for the pigs, built around regular daily food distribution and frequent movements to new paddocks, which are able to be quickly reconfigured with portable electric fencing and water troughs. Unlike their intensive counterparts, there is a complete absence of routine surgical interventions such as teeth clipping, tail docking and castration. The Hicks place a high priority on maintaining the calmest possible environment — partly because relaxed pigs are a joy to be around, while distressed pigs certainly aren't, but also because a calm pig will be naturally healthier and yield more tender, flavoursome meat.

The sweet prospect of the apple is the pig's last conscious desire before being swiftly stunned, bled and killed.

Let's talk

With all of this in mind, and in a bid to close the production loop, in 2017 Michael and Alex embarked on the building of a portable, on-farm abattoir. With the assistance of limited dollar-for-dollar state government funding, they modified a retired shipping container to suit their needs, introducing a clever design innovation that reduced the footprint of the abattoir structure. Michael proved himself adept at meeting the complex engineering challenges of the project.

Crucially, Michael also undertook training to become a qualified meat inspector, able to assess and pass the pigs slaughtered on-farm as being fit for human consumption, a vital component in the paddock-to-plate chain, and possibly the main stumbling block for anyone considering on-farm slaughter. Transport to Sydney courtesy of a local farmer-owned refrigerated delivery truck that picks up directly from the farm means that all the key components of the enterprise are now contained and managed onsite.

The Hicks process their pigs fortnightly, and rarely do more than 10–12 pigs in a day. To put this in context, a commercial abattoir will process hundreds or even thousands of pigs per day. Every abattoir is given a unique number, and at Extraordinary Pork, every carcass carrying that number was bred, raised and processed on the farm. This is genuinely an extraordinary fact. First, these pigs are already among a minority because only about 3 per cent of Australian pigs are born and bred at farms on which they are free to range on pasture for their entire lives. Second, because as far as we know, Extraordinary Pork is currently the only pasture-raised pig farm in New South Wales, probably the entire country, with the capacity to breed, pasture-raise and process entirely on farm. This offers manifold benefits for the animals, the farmers, the environment, and for us — the consumers of the final product.

Given that we're talking about slaughter, it may sound strange to say that the Extraordinary Pork process is extraordinarily calm, quiet and, yes, humane. The evening before, the pigs literally walk straight from the paddock to an overnight holding pen. Then, in the morning, the pen gate is opened and they amble down a dirt road (see photo on page 70) to the lairage — the small, shaded area in front of the abattoir where the animal waits. The aim is for the pigs' gastrointestinal tract to be largely empty at the time of slaughter, to minimise the possibility of faecal contamination of the carcass. After an hour or so to acclimatise to their lairage, the first pig is gently ushered around a curving, low-walled corridor. On the ground, a metre or so in front of the pig, is a solitary apple. Unable to resist it, the pig steps forward and the sweet prospect of the apple becomes its last conscious desire, as it is then swiftly stunned before being quickly bled and killed.

Building and operating an on-farm abattoir is not simply an exercise in improving logistics and reducing the stress experienced by the pigs prior to slaughter. The animals at Extraordinary Pork are purposefully bred and raised for food, and their deaths, well before senescence would ordinarily claim them, are clearly premature. Producers like Michael and Alex Hicks recognise that the pact they enter into is a solemn one. The images here clearly show the intimate scale of the operation.

But, more importantly, we hope what they also show is recognition of the responsibility that comes with the giving and taking of life. As retailers or consumers of animals for food, it is our duty to support the systems in which that recognition is central.

It is our hope that what is extraordinary now becomes ordinary in the future.

Opposite top: *Extraordinary Pork abattoir, built inside a recycled container with a door from Sydney's Star Casino.*
Opposite bottom left: *Michael Hicks inside the abbatoir.*
Opposite bottom right: *Each carcass is stamped with the unique Extraordinary Pork abattoir number.*

These are carefully managed human–animal interactions that require thought and careful observation and practice to get right. And often, it's what you *don't* do that makes the difference. Ask anyone who handles dairy cows who gets to organise the milking roster, and they'll tell you it's the cows themselves that decide, with all the bossy matrons right up the front!

Temple Grandin, an American professor of animal science — portrayed in a 2010 biopic starring Claire Danes — has written many books detailing her profound insights on how to think like a cow, or sheep, or pig. Her designs and strategies for minimising distress for animals prior to and during slaughter have been adopted by many abattoirs around the world. By understanding what a cow is attracted to, and what may frighten or alarm it, or how a pig doesn't like to queue, or what level of noise will make a sheep stop in its tracks, Grandin's ideas have been instrumental in greatly improving the way in which the majority of animals are slaughtered.

Some of her improvements are as simple as moving a light source so it doesn't have reflections visible at the eye level of a pig. Sometimes it will require completely redesigning the lairage, or implementing ways to accurately monitor stunning efficiency, or measuring the frequency of strongly coercive behaviour employed by staff. In all of these cases, economic self-interest overlaps with animal welfare imperatives, given that better-quality meat is simply worth more.

Arriving at the abattoir: a licence to kill

When the stock truck arrives at the abattoir, a pen is allocated, and the animals are unloaded. It is infinitely preferable that the penning precludes mixing with other animals, as it takes about 3 weeks to establish a new pecking order in a cow herd, and some older sheep may never 'flock up', even if their offspring will. It is far better that the animals that were reared together and travelled together are penned together. Which, by the way, is why we always try to avoid having an animal sent to the abattoir by itself. A cow or sheep or goat is part of a herd or flock, and the herd or flock logic is that there is safety in numbers and if you are separated from the herd you won't last long. All of these animals are

'For the most part the meat commodity market only rewards a single attribute: weight.'

herbivores and are preyed upon in the wild, and occasionally on the farm as well. Despite centuries of domestication and selective breeding, that awareness is still deeply embedded in their psyche, and is at the heart of Grandin's insights into their behaviour.

Most of the animals we source go through the abattoirs as a so-called 'private kill' and are booked in by the producer, with the carcasses consigned directly to us as the end customer. This means that we are not purchasing from the abattoir itself, which will often market meat under its own brand(s) as well. The meat offered by the abattoir will be a collection of what has been bought from the sale yards, most likely from a variety of producers, or occasionally purchased directly, in large numbers as a single order from a single farm. Having all the sale animals leave the farm in one or two deliveries suits some larger producers as it allows them to plan their production with more predictable revenues, even if the price is determined more by the market, which may or may not equate with what may be considered a fair return for the quality of the animals supplied — making them price-takers rather than price-setters.

One of the great inequities of the commodity market, which accounts for most of the meat sold in Australia, is that for the most part it only rewards a single attribute: weight. But as we have already seen, meat is the embodiment of so many other attributes that are embedded in the product itself — some measurable, such as nutrient quality, and some more subjective, like depth and persistence of flavour. How can one account for these qualities if you only have the blunt instrument of the scale to determine value?

Dissatisfaction with this arrangement leads some producers to partner with a butchery like ours, where the benefits of mutually agreed prices and farm branding outweigh the increased logistical difficulties that regular and/or frequent supply entails. We can reliably detail a particular farmer's practice — all of the things that may distinguish them from any other farmer — even if that other farmer may be their immediate neighbour. When a producer does enter into a supply relationship with us, the abattoir is being privately contracted to provide killing and freight delivery services. The key difference here is that both the premises in which the slaughter is carried out, and the meat inspector who finally assesses the carcass, are *licensed* and independently audited by a branch of the Department of Primary Industries. (Only poultry is exempt from the requirement of having a meat inspector present to assess each carcass, which is why there are many more on-farm poultry abattoirs, which are instead subject to periodic audits from the state licensing authority.)

While Robert's father was able to slaughter a sheep for on-farm consumption, the wrath of the state's food authority would descend on him if he attempted to sell that meat to his neighbour. It is only when a licensed inspector has passed a particular carcass fit for human consumption that the familiar red vegetable dye marks are stamped or rolled onto its flank, carrying a numbered code that allows traceability back to the abattoir, and a code or name based on a prior assessment of the animal's teeth, the numbers of which accurately reflect the animal's age at slaughter.

As all of the 'private kills' are done at the start of the day — as are any 'certified organic' kills that the abattoir may be licensed for — there is the distinct advantage of less time waiting in the yards, which translates into less stress for the animals. It has also been shown (Grandin again) that the efficiency and accuracy of operators on the kill floor declines after 2 hours, so being included in the early morning shift is a double bonus and likely to produce the best possible outcome.

It should be noted that not all abattoirs are licensed to kill all animals. Some are licensed for a single species, which is often the case for chickens or birds in general — and many don't kill pigs at all, as a different production line is needed to process their carcasses. As pigs, like chickens, are sold skin-on, they have their hair removed by immersion in a scald bath where the pigs are rotated in water kept at 64°C for 4–5 minutes. Flexible rubber paddles scrape the hair off, or in the case of chickens, their feathers.

Pigs and chickens aside, all the other animals we source are stripped of their hide, which will find its way to the leather industry, as just one of the supply contracts an abattoir will have for a dizzying array of manufactured products, all or partially derived from animal sources — anything from soap to adhesives, emery boards to shampoo, guitar strings to fine bone china. Truly, nothing is wasted, and for the larger commercial abattoirs these by-products are vital contributors to their overall profitability.

Occasionally we have the hides processed ourselves, turning the winter hide of a spectacular 4-year-old Belted Galloway or Scottish Highland steer into a striking and durable floor rug. This involves the skins being recovered directly from the abattoir, immediately after slaughter, where they are thickly coated in salt and weigh close to 80 kilograms. After five days of salting, they're ready to be sent to Greenhalgh Tannery near Ballarat in Victoria, the last commercial tannery in Australia still working with traditional slow cures. Their leather is still cured with black-wattle bark, and their hides with minimal chromium, taking close to four weeks as opposed to the standard three days in a conventional tannery. The current owners, brothers Ross and Bruce, are the fifth generation to manage their business, and probably the last, as their sons and daughters are unlikely to be taking over. Unfortunately, artisan curing has largely been superseded by quicker, but more toxic, chemical processes.

It is a source of continuing frustration that we can't make more use of the hides of the animals that we buy, but if we thought dealing in meat with guaranteed provenance had its challenges, it's nothing compared to the diminishing options of bespoke leather tanning.

A stunning prelude to death

While different species are handled by different abattoirs, what is common to all facilities is that the animal, whether it's a chicken or a pig, a cow or a sheep, is stunned, rendering the animal unconscious, and in some cases already dead, prior to being bled. Stunning can be achieved through an electrical charge, carbon dioxide gas or captive bolt projectile, all of which will be discussed in detail below. The only exception that we are aware of in Australia is for animals destined for Kosher butchers, which we believe are still required to be fully conscious when bled. We receive Halal-certified meat (beef, lamb and goat) from two different abattoirs. The standards for Halal certification are set by the Australian National Imams Council (ANIC) and, contrary to popular belief, allow for an animal to be temporarily stunned prior to slaughter. That is, the stunned animal should be capable of regaining consciousness, and this capacity is required to be checked at regular intervals throughout the day.

This point about animals being rendered unconscious before slaughter is important — as it is sometimes claimed that animals, usually pigs, are gassed to death, asphyxiated in the oxygen-depleted, carbon dioxide–rich atmosphere of a small chamber. Carbon dioxide chambers are commonly used to stun pigs because, as previously noted, pigs don't like to queue, but prefer to enter a space shoulder to shoulder with other pigs. (Possibly this feels more natural to them as they may be one of 14(!) piglets born in a litter, and lining up, side by side for a drink at their mother's teat, is the first thing they know of the outside world.)

In our experience, only gentle direction is required for several pigs (usually three or four, depending on size) to enter the chamber together. As carbon dioxide is heavier than air, the chamber then rotates or sinks to a lower

'Both meat quality and shelf life are reliant on effective bleeding out of the carcass.'

level where the concentration of the gas should reach around 90 per cent. However, carbon dioxide is an aversive gas, discernible to the animal in high concentrations. Testing shows it takes 9–12 seconds from when the pigs are able to detect the high level of carbon dioxide before they are rendered unconscious by it, and it is during this period that pigs, especially those already distressed from poor handling, will struggle to escape the oxygen-depleted environment.

When the chamber rises and the door opens, there are the three or four unconscious pigs, lying on their sides. Speed in the operation is now essential, as there is limited time before the pigs may regain consciousness.

In most cases they will be shackled by the hind leg and lifted onto a moving overhead chain. The slaughterman will pierce the carotid artery along with the other major blood vessels leading from the heart, and the unconscious pig dies while hanging upside down, its blood pumped out by its own still-beating heart. Both meat quality and shelf life are reliant on effective bleeding out of the carcass, or 'exsanguination' as it is known in the scientific literature.

Like people, pigs have markedly different reactions to the presence of elevated levels of carbon dioxide, and in both cases strong adverse reactions are largely genetically determined. Pigs carrying a particular gene that is usually present in a strain of the Hampshire breed, common in America but much less so in Australia, are predisposed to react much more strongly to the gas. Testing on turkeys has shown that argon, either by itself or mixed with carbon dioxide, would be preferable as it is essentially non-aversive and not detected by the animals exposed to it before they lose consciousness. We believe that further testing using non-aversive gas for different species should be carried out to determine their relative effectiveness. While the incidence of strongly aversive behaviours such as excessive vocalisation and panicked movements may be rare, informing ourselves of what methods abattoirs use for both stunning and slaughter, and what the consequences of these methods are, allows us to demand of those who kill in our name that their practices are of the highest possible standard, including the use of non-aversive gas.

While we recognise that many abattoirs already struggle to be commercially viable, exploring the options and additional expense of using non-aversive gases such as argon really should be high on the list of improvements that can be made in the slaughter process.

As a side note, in our home state of New South Wales, pig producers located on or near the state's mid-north coast now have a minimum five-hour journey either north or south to access licensed abattoir services. The greater the distance that animals are transported to slaughter, the greater the negative impact on the animal and the resultant meat quality. This example reflects a wider problem of abattoir consolidation, with many closures in the last 10 years alone. Some of these abattoirs may reopen, but with a reduced range of animals that can be processed, or possibly an exclusive focus on meat destined for export.

Delivering the electrical charge

With chickens, sheep, goats and some pigs, electrical stunning is commonly used. While electrical stunning is favoured by Grandin as the most effective of all methods on larger animals, there is greater potential for operator error — from inaccurate placement of the electrodes on the sides of the animal's head, to incorrect activation of the charge with the appropriate voltage, frequency and amperage for the size of the animal being stunned. In all of these cases, when done correctly, a generalised tonic–clonic (grand mal) seizure is induced. The animal is then tested for a corneal reflex, confirming loss of consciousness if the eye can be touched without response.

Sometimes a heart stun is applied following the head stun — the advantage being that the first charge does not need to be as strong, and the resultant meat quality is improved. This second charge also stops the heart beating for at least 5 seconds, ensuring the animal is brain-dead when being bled out. Another benefit is that there is a marked reduction in jerky leg movements, and accurate 'sticking' (piercing the carotid artery and severing the blood vessels leading from the heart) is easier, with more efficient bleeding the result. The expression 'to squeal like a stuck pig' betrays poor slaughter practice, as voluntary vocalisation, in any species, is a sure sign of incomplete or non-existent stunning.

In the case of chickens (and ducks), the most common method — and one employed by the organic chicken processor we source from — is where the chicken is suspended by its feet on a moving line. When chickens are hung upside down they quieten and relax, and unlike other species rarely attempt to lift their heads, allowing the head of the chicken to pass through a water bath that carries an electrical current strong enough to render the bird unconscious, but not so strong that the bird dies. The bird is subsequently bled and dies while still suspended.

And finally, to cattle and very large pigs. These animals are rendered insensible with a captive-bolt gun — a high-powered device that uses compressed air to fire a steel bolt that either penetrates the skull and immediately retracts, causing irreparable damage to the brain and killing the animal, or a non-penetrative mushroom-head bolt that renders the animal unconscious from the powerful percussive blow.

Accuracy in placement and angle of approach are critical to the success of these methods, as are the specially designed 'knocking boxes' — metal stalls that gently squeeze the animal on both sides and lift the head high in a head bail, which serves to keep the animal almost motionless. This allows the operator to achieve the very high rates of insensibility that studies show can be produced by these two methods. Occasionally, possibly due to malfunctioning equipment or poor technique on the part of the operator, an additional shot may be required, and a second device is always kept nearby for that purpose. In the case of the penetrative bolt, mild electrical stimulation will be applied to the body to keep the heart pumping so that bleeding will still occur efficiently.

Anything less than 100 per cent insensibility prior to slaughter is lamentable and, it must be said, unacceptable. The whole purpose of these systems is to minimise the suffering and stress that may be associated with the killing of animals, which as we have seen, has significant welfare, quality and therefore cost implications. When someone close to us dies unexpectedly, say in an accident, we will commiserate with each other over the loss, and if it was a quick death, console ourselves with the idea that our friend, or partner, or family member, didn't suffer — and that, at least, is something for which we should be grateful. We should wish the same for the animals that die in our name.

> '**The purpose of these systems is to minimise the suffering and stress associated with killing animals.**'

Transforming the carcass

Having died, the animal is only now at the beginning of the next stage, where it is transformed into food. It is reported that Henry Ford revolutionised car manufacture and conceived the assembly plant by watching the *dis*-assembly of animals being processed in an abattoir — an example of early specialisation where each worker on the abattoir line had a specific job. And with each worker performing their specialised operation, an entire animal is deftly and swiftly transformed into a carcass. Aside from pigs and chickens where the animal is kept whole, the hide, head and feet are removed, the animal is eviscerated, and the major organs identified with a number that matches the carcass, so when it reaches the meat inspector, who is last in the disassembly line, an accurate assessment can be made of the health of the animal. Any evidence of disease the animal may have suffered will show up in the heart, the kidneys and the liver, and can be closely assessed. At this point an inspector may condemn any or all of the offal, or order the removal of a limb if there is evidence of arthritis or a break.

Depending on the animal, different parts will be removed prior to assessment — feet, head, viscera and hide in the case of ruminants, and hair, toenails and viscera for pigs. Chickens will usually have their head and feathers removed, but some are sold with their head and feet still attached. The 'dressed weight' of the carcass can be as low as 45 per cent of the live body weight in the case of goats, right up to 76 per cent for pigs, and is known as the dressing percentage. Certain breeds of cattle like Speckle Park or Dexter may be favoured because they have a higher dressing percentage and/or a higher ratio of muscle to bone.

If the inspector is happy with the condition of both the carcass and the offal, the carcass will be affixed with a vegetable-dye stamp familiar to anyone who has ever bought a rack of lamb. It must now undergo chilling at a speed that is rapid enough to ensure meat quality, but not so fast that the muscles are 'cold shortened' by the too-rapid expulsion of calcium from the muscle fibres. Every carcass will undergo shrinkage in this process, and in the case of a large body of beef that may be as much as 8 kilograms. Generally, we pay the producer for

'Hopefully most of you who set off on this journey are still with us.'

the 'hot weight' of the carcass, but obviously only receive the cold weight when delivered — an anomaly that is accepted within the industry.

The idea of all chilling systems is for the meat to be lowered to storage temperature with a corresponding drop in pH to the desirable level of 5.5 or 5.6 from a live level of 7.4 in the same timeframe. Too quick or slow a drop in pH or temperature will have dramatic impacts on meat quality, colour and shelf life.

Once all these criteria have been met, the carcass will be delivered to our cool room, often in the dead of night. Avoiding peak-hour city traffic if you're driving a semi-trailer is definitely an advantage, and all of Sydney's meat carters have a locksmith's collection of keys to every cool room in the city. We ask for the offal to come with each carcass, but only occasionally do we receive all of the offal we would like. Depending on the animal this will include the tongue, brain, liver, kidneys, heart and tail, all of which have fans amongst our customers. Sourcing other organs is a little trickier, and some are completely unobtainable as they will be sent straight from the abattoir to a third-party processor.

Take the case of intestines, which we exclusively use for all of our sausages. You can use skins manufactured from collagen, but they are disturbingly straight, with no gentle natural curve, and have a disconcerting 'squeaky' bite that we don't favour. As far as we know, there is only one factory left in Australia still processing intestines for sausage skins, and they only process lamb, which we use for our thin sausages (22–24 millimetre diameter). All of our thick sausages (26–28 millimetre diameter) are made using hog (pig) casings, and all of those available in Australia are processed in China — although presumably a small percentage of them are derived from animals that lived and died in Australia, their intestines making the round trip, albeit minus the sightseeing.

We are as dependent on the meat carter as a commercial kitchen is on its kitchen hands. Unsung and largely unrecognised, these men — and they are exclusively men in our experience — may load and unload tens of tonnes of meat each and every day using only their guile and strength. We salute them and acknowledge that a business like ours that exclusively sources meat on the bone wouldn't last long without their herculean efforts, and this is our chance to thank them.

Once safely arrived, these carcasses of animals as young as eight weeks in the case of birds and suckling pigs, and anything up to 7–8 years old in the case of long-retired cows, will jostle for space and demand a different sort of attention and treatment. Mature beef and sheep meat may be aged further — for anything up to eight weeks — coaxing tenderness from oft-used muscles, and complex, deep and sometimes truly profound flavours, from the unknowable interplay of enzyme and matter, infused with the essence of place.

Hopefully most of you who set off on this journey are still with us. We field so many questions about how the organised killing of animals is conducted that it is our fervent hope that staring at the bright light of slaughter and understanding even a little of how the process actually works will help to place this fatal moment in context.

Killing should never be taken lightly. It is no small thing. The best abattoirs understand that they have a community responsibility and operate with a social licence that is constantly in need of review. And we understand that we also operate with a licence that is only granted to us by our customers, who trust us to engage as honestly as we can with the grim and glorious realities of life and death.

As farmer Joel Salatin reminded us at the beginning of this chapter, this process of killing animals, if it is to be done well, must be based on respect. Both for the animals we husband and kill for food, and ultimately for ourselves.

Butcher Will Heath, representing the next generation of artisan, whole-body butchers.

5.

The whole animal and nothing but the animal

The dying art of whole-animal butchery

Butchery is a beautiful and venerable craft, and when it is performed with expertise it is full of respect for the life given up to feed us. As long as we continue to eat animals, we need skilled and caring people to prepare our meat for us.

Let's talk

After a slightly rocky start during which our delivery service may have included yoga blankets and an old Toyota Corolla sedan, and we may have sold a three-legged lamb that should have had four legs to a two-hat chef desperate for three hats, we found our feet in the world of butchery and fell in love with the beauty and craft of this rich, visceral world.

Filled with crusading zeal for a better food model, we decided that our commitment to transparency and a whole-animal practice meant two things. First, we would seek out diverse breeds of animals grown on farms managed with the goal of improving the entire ecosystem. Second, we wouldn't buy boxed meat from a wholesaler, but instead would always buy meat on the bone direct from the farmer, offal and all, or in isolated cases from their nominated representative.

Meat as a commodity

Traditional whole-animal butcheries have become a rarity in many developed countries. A butchery business model organised around specific parameters such as sourcing whole, pasture-raised animals direct from the farmer forces the butcher to operate outside of the mainstream meat marketplace — a choice that is considered contrary and eccentric. The overwhelming majority of domestic and export meat in Australia is traded through the commodity meat market. If you doubt this, take a peek at the futures market for meat, where billions of dollars are traded on animals that are yet to be born. It's a game for the big guys in which the volumes are measured in thousands of tonnes, and product differentiation isn't a factor.

Left: *Meat carter, Andrew 'Spider' Byrnes. Meat carters load and unload tonnes of meat every single day using only their guile and strength. A business like ours that exclusively sources meat on the bone wouldn't last long without their herculean efforts.*

Much of the meat produced for this market will be sourced from farms that are organised around the primary goal of maximising turnover of animals. The management strategies at the farms that feed into this market include breeding specifically for fast growth and high yield, often confining animals to feedlots or sheds — so-called 'concentrated animal feeding operations', or CAFOs — while incorporating sub-therapeutic antibiotic medication into their feed, as well as hormones to promote growth. As a system that rewards volume and speed, it works brilliantly.

'We enjoy the profit, convenience and low prices, trusting that someone else will deal with the problems.'

But if you're a farmer or butcher or consumer interested in other dimensions of value, such as traceable animal and environmental welfare standards, or an animal's nutritional density (greatly determined by the health of the ecosystem in which it has lived), then it will come up short. This is because when a farmer sells into the mainstream commodity market, their animals disappear into a generic product pool. There is rarely any recognition of the nuances in different farm management systems or different breeds, the price fluctuates according to external pressures that have little to do with a farmer's practice, the animals are broken down and sold to retail butchers in boxed sections, and the farmer has no idea who ends up eating their produce. In this system, smaller-scale farmers are price-takers, forced to accept what is offered, rather than being price-setters.

Of course, just because something is produced at a large scale doesn't mean that quality, ethics and animal, human and environmental welfare are automatically compromised. This is where regulations, the implementation of industry standards that match community expectations, and certification schemes such as organics become so important. But if a business is sourcing produce from 10 different farms to sell under a single brand and not providing the consumer with information about those farms, then the connection between producer and consumer is broken. The potential for building knowledge and accountability on both sides is diminished. The farmer doesn't know where their animals will end up and who will eat them, and the end consumer is similarly ignorant about the source of the food they are eating, and the methods employed to grow it. This applies equally to grain and legume production. Choosing a vegetarian or vegan diet won't necessarily guarantee a more benevolent or transparent source.

Despite the growing indications that things might not be going as smoothly as we'd hoped, we're all charging ahead enjoying the profit, convenience and low prices, trusting that someone else will deal with the problems.

In the world of butchery, the commodity system holds fast. Meat retailing is increasingly polarised between a super-cheap, super-generic offer at one end, and a 'gourmet' offer at the other. Many people buy their meat at supermarkets, meaning the traditional high-street retail butcher, unable to compete, is starting to go the way of newsagents. (Remember newsagents?)

One way to maintain commercial relevance and imbue the trade with meaning is to practise whole-animal butchery — but very few retail butchers buy whole animals because it has become a trickier and riskier endeavour. You need room to hang the carcasses, the skills to break down the body, and you must sell the whole body, or a significant proportion of it, to make a living. Instead, as we've seen, most butchers buy their meat in boxes of plastic-wrapped carcass sections that they break down into the familiar cuts that consumers want to buy. Larger butchery operations do buy whole animals, but the majority of the meat they source will arrive in boxes.

Meat in a box

There are lots of compelling advantages to boxed meat. Boxes are easy to store and, because the meat 'wet ages' in plastic, there isn't any loss from dry ageing. (We'll explain dry ageing in more detail later in this chapter.) Boxes allow the butcher the freedom to only buy the sections of the carcass that they are pretty confident they can sell, the sorts of cuts that customers ask for and are familiar with — slow-cooking cuts in the cooler months, fast cooking in the warmer months. This limits the risk of waste, which is the enemy of profit.

But boxed meat has its limitations. By only responding to consumer demand, the butcher isn't shaping or extending the customer's desire, capacity or knowledge. In fact, like the algorithms that determine our social media feeds, each time you select a cut, you're reinforcing the supply of that cut and potentially narrowing the range of available choices. In addition, the butcher is usually buying their meat from an intermediary, whose word is often the only thing they have to go by when it comes to checking the authenticity of the product. They're unlikely to have a personal relationship with the farmer, to have visited the farm or know much about how the animals were raised. They may not know how they were transported when they left the farm gate, and they're unlikely to have visited the abattoir or have a relationship with the managers. When the box arrives with the plastic-packed meat inside, the butcher has very limited information about the meat, so it's difficult to verify provenance or manage quality control. In the case of skinned animals such as sheep, sometimes the boxed muscles have also had the fat removed, which makes this even harder. In these cases, substitution of lamb with hogget (older, less commercially valuable sheep) is rife.

So, in the vast majority of cases, boxed meat is literally a disembodied commodity that offers the butcher a relatively narrow range of creative potential, and very little by which to gauge its worth beyond what they paid for it and how it looks. There isn't much of a story the butcher can tell their customers about her product, which makes for a rather dull exchange, but it's definitely efficient and business-like. Keep it simple, give customers what they want, manage costs and minimise the risk of waste.

If you're doubtful about this, try asking your local butcher or the sales staff at your local supermarket some of the questions our customers ask us every day about the meat we sell.

- Which farm does this meat come from?
- Where is it located — have you been there?
- How is it managed?
- What is the stocking density?
- What is the difference between Free Range, Pasture Raised, Grass Fed, Organic and Biodynamic?
- Are chemicals used on the farm — pesticides, herbicides, fungicides, chemical fertilisers, antibiotics, growth promotants?
- What breed is the animal — why did the farmer choose the breed?
- How was it raised?
- What did it eat?
- If it ate grain, did that grain include genetically modified crops?
- Why do you sell veal — isn't it unethical?
- How old was the animal at slaughter?
- How was it transported to the abattoir?
- How was it killed?
- When was it killed?
- What happens when meat is dry aged, and why do you do it?

'Buying whole animals direct from the grower opens up a whole world of connection and complexity.'

If they can answer half of those questions, and you're sure they're not just telling you what they think you want to hear, then you're on to a good thing and you should stick with them!

Meat out of the box

Compared to buying boxed meat from an intermediary, buying whole animals direct from the grower opens up a whole world of stories, connection, complexity and responsibility. It's a riskier business, but far more interesting and rewarding.

For us, the whole process starts long before we get involved, and sometimes it's hard to say where exactly it begins and ends. Sometimes we think it begins with the arrival of a litter of piglets destined for our cool room, born in a nest built by a determined, single-minded sow, sited wherever she decided was best, which may or may not be where the farmer thinks is most appropriate. But perhaps it starts before that, when the sow herself was born. Sometimes we think it ends when the last gram of meat from an animal is sold in our butchery. But then, when our customers bring their kids into the butchery, some of whom we've known since they were born, we decide that, actually, this is where it ends, one animal absorbing another and continuing the cycle of life. It's a privilege to be trusted with the job of playing a small part in those lives, the animal and the child.

Whatever the animal, when it arrives at our butchery, we know a lot about where it comes from, how it was produced, how it died and how it arrived at our door, and this, we believe, is as it should be — because buying whole animals directly from the farmer brings everyone into the loop, and connects us all the way back to the soil, and all the way forward to the plate on the table. Connection creates communities; communities foster accountability. The more we know each other, the more we care and the stronger we are.

Of course, if your business is built around buying the whole animal, then you also have to *sell* the whole animal, which can be challenging. Many of us have lost the traditional skills that allowed us to prepare and consume the whole animal.

'How do you cook skirt? What do you do with oyster blade? What about heart, liver or tongue?'

Eating offal was something quaint our grandparents did, and these days we spend more time watching cooking shows than we actually do preparing food. All of this means we default to the cuts we know how to cook, and we're less likely to choose the less familiar ones.

Take an average beef carcass, for example. The 2–3-year-old cattle that we buy direct from the farm usually weigh in at 300+ kilograms carcass weight. About 25 per cent of the carcass yields the primary cuts that most people know and feel comfortable cooking — eye fillet, sirloin, rump. To put that in context, eye fillet makes up about 1.3 per cent of the entire carcass, so we'd suggest that it should only be eaten 1.3 per cent of the time. Another 25 per cent of the carcass offers equally familiar secondary cuts such as minute steaks, chuck and blade. But the remaining 50 per cent of the carcass is comprised of bones, fat, offal and muscles that are delicious when properly trimmed and prepared, but aren't part of the usual domestic cook's repertoire. How do you cook skirt? (Astonishingly, a first year Australian butchery apprentice is taught that 'skirt' is only good for trim, but our customers know that skirt is a delicious cut that also happens to be a staple of Asian and South American cuisine. See page 132 for a great recipe.) What do you do with oyster blade? What about heart, liver or tongue? We can turn a fair bit of that remaining 50 per cent into familiar products like dice, mince, sausages and broth, but if we're going to pay proper dues to the life given up to feed us and not waste a thing, then customers need to be persuaded to jump in the deep end and try new cuts. Fortunately, our customers are gutsy, adventurous, creative and endlessly curious. As you can see from their recipes in this book, there are many ways to eat the whole animal.

The eight-legged cow and the miracle of the Christmas ham

The other challenge in whole-animal butchery is the fact that we're stuck with what nature has given each animal we sell. We've been lobbying all the available divinities for years, but so far our prayers haven't been answered, and the mythical beast that in winter grows eight legs (for extra osso buco), four tails (for extra oxtail) and four heads (for extra beef cheeks), and in summer sheds eight legs (no one wants osso buco in summer) and grows four extra loins (for steaks) hasn't transpired. This can be a real problem for the whole-animal butcher.

Then there's the miracle of the Christmas ham.

Like all butchers in Western countries, each December we sell hundreds of whole hams. There are usually two ways for butchers to manage this explosive, one-off spike in demand. They either buy bulk boxes of anonymous pig legs from the commodity market, or they squirrel away the legs from the whole pigs they buy each week throughout the year. As we've seen, not many butchers buy whole pigs, so the second option is the less travelled path. In our case, the hams we offer are made exclusively from the legs of the pasture-raised pigs we source each week from regeneratively managed farms in New South Wales. Pigs raised this way — born and bred on pasture and regularly rotated to fresh paddocks with mobile shelters — make up only 3 per cent of the Australian pork meat trade, so there's a limited number of legs available for curing. Each week we cure some legs from these whole pigs to meet the weekly demand for ham, and the remaining legs we stockpile for Christmas. Which leaves the remainder of the pig that needs to be sold each week as fresh pork cuts to our regular customers who buy weekly or fortnightly, although a good percentage of the belly and loin will also be cured for bacon.

As soon as we open up Christmas orders, our customer base balloons and we are overwhelmed by the responsibility of making sure that everyone gets exactly what they need for their big event. Then, when the party's over, many of those customers disappear until next Christmas and we remember that this happens every year. We're not complaining. Many customers only shop with us at Christmas time and we are grateful and proud that they return to us for their annual celebratory ham. It's a special occasion and it's wonderful that they care enough to want a high-welfare, high-quality ham. But the thing is, if you want to continue to eat a high-welfare, good-quality ham at Christmas time, then you may need to buy high-welfare, good-quality pork more than once a year, so the farms that are growing to the standards you admire are able to survive.

If there were more consistent demand for pasture-raised pork, there would probably be more farms growing it.

Extraordinary times call for extraordinary measures

We've only broken our cardinal rule of never buying boxed meat once, and we did it in spectacular style, receiving a single delivery of most of a mob of organic Wagyu steers, neatly packed into 146 boxes. It was extremely unnerving to see the delivery truck doors open on pallet-loads of boxes, rather than the usual whole carcasses broken into the halves or quarters that we're so proud to hang in our cool room, and it took a lot of navel-gazing and gin for us to arrive at that point.

Australia's annual fire season is becoming progressively longer and more ferocious as climate change starts to bite and, despite the work they do to mitigate against the impacts of climate change, regenerative farmers are as vulnerable as anyone else. In 2017, Gundooee Organics, a Wagyu beef farm we've sourced from for over 10 years, was razed by a savage fire that tore through the district, destroying the farm's infrastructure and all the precious grasses to feed the pasture-raised cattle. Owner Rob Lennon proudly refused our offers to run a fundraiser but he did ask us to immediately buy 22 large, 3–4-year-old cattle — he needed funds for recovery. For us, this wasn't a straightforward exercise. To start with, the only abattoir within a viable distance with the infrastructure to handle big cattle is an export-geared abattoir with a minimum order of 20 carcasses per customer. Regulations prohibit the export of whole carcasses on the bone and only boned, boxed meat is permitted for export. So the only way to make this work was for us to break our 10-year whole-animal record, receive the cattle in boxes and take the lot in one delivery. For years, every month like clockwork, we'd bought carcasses of Rob's wonderful 2–3-year-old Wagyu cattle, which we'd dry-age and sell progressively over 6 weeks — very paced and very considered. So to buy 22 in one delivery was a big disruption to that rhythm.

But these were extraordinary circumstances. Once we'd worked out the logistics, we realised that it was a rare opportunity to handle older Wagyu beef from one of the best growers in the country. In Australia, most beef comes from cattle that are bred and fed to reach market size within 15 months, and the resulting 'yearling' beef is relatively flavourless compared to beef from more

'A good butcher has a surgeon's understanding of physiology and an artist's imagination.'

mature animals. But because consumers are consistently presented with meat that is becoming softer and less flavoursome, this is what people now expect. By comparison, older cattle are considered tough and attract a lower market price, so there is little financial incentive for farmers to 'grow out' their animals, which just reinforces the trend towards an increasingly bland product range.

The point of this story is that we were able to buy and sell Rob's older beef to an appreciative audience because it has never been treated as a commodity by him, by us, or by our customers. Everyone, at every point in the production and consumption cycle, understands that Gundooee beef, like everything we sell, is a manifestation of soil, seasons, farming practice, genetics, animal handling, and slaughter and butchery techniques. You're not just buying a product, be it meat or potatoes or lentils or milk — you're casting a vote for a production system and the sort of world in which you want to live.

So, when the big back doors of the delivery truck open and the meat carter rattles down the ramp and into our cool room, bowed under the weight of a carcass, we already know a lot about the animal. We've visited the farms over different seasons so we understand the specific characteristics of the place and, depending on when we last visited the farm, we may have seen the same animals running around in the paddock before we see their carcasses hanging in our cool room. We've had many lengthy discussions with the farmer about the conditions of the season, the animals, the farm and any number of other related subjects, and we've often visited the abattoirs at which these animals were processed and watched the kill when permitted.

At this point, with the whole animal hanging on hooks in one, two, four or occasionally eight parts in our cool room, with the offal in a box alongside, the carcass reveals a wealth of information about genetics, the season, the energy and protein levels of the feed, and the quality of the slaughter process. We are the eyes of the farmer, and we report back regarding the carcass quality, fat levels, muscle conformation and carcass handling. The condition of the delivered carcass also dictates how we store, break and sell the carcass, in particular the amount of time we allow it to hang. This is where the skill and craft of butchery comes to the fore.

The dying art of butchery

Puns aside, this is a serious subject. We think that butchery is a beautiful and venerable craft, and when it is performed with skilful expertise it is full of respect and admiration for the life given up to feed us. As long as we continue to eat animals, we need skilled and caring people to prepare our meat for us.

Unfortunately, in many parts of the developed world, butchery knowledge is slowly being lost and the trade is declining, because the commodity meat market requires less skill, so fewer and fewer people are taking up the knives. This loss of skill and craft is largely due to the rapid consolidation of the meat industry. When most meat arrives as dissected primal cuts vacuum-packed in plastic in a box, there's no requirement for the butcher to understand the wealth of information provided by a whole carcass, or to know the most elegant and efficient way to break the whole body down to limit waste, maximise yield or allow for careful dry ageing. When you're not forced to find ways to encourage your customers to cook the whole body, you forget how to do it yourself. When you can stuff your sausages with fillers, flavour enhancers and preservatives, you forget how to make fresh, hand-made sausages with natural ingredients. When the meat you're sourcing is immature, undifferentiated by breed or production process and relatively bland, most of your effort goes into jazzing it up with pre-prepared commercial marinades and spice mixes.

Our butchers understand that when the meat is intrinsically good, you don't need to do much, either in the cutting or the cooking. Trimming well is the secret and a well-cut piece of meat will cook better and is preferable to tricked-up products. Then there's the perception that butchery is a hard, thankless and slightly unpalatable business that most of us are glad is done by someone else. It's true that it's a hard, physical job and there are blood and guts involved. You need to love the feeling of being physically exhausted at the end of the day if you're going to be a butcher.

But butchery can also be meditative and creative, and is a critical link in the chain that feeds us. There are days when we walk through the cool room and the production area and we are awestruck by the visceral beauty and gravity of what we do every day. The cool room, with its clean, slightly iron smell, is a quiet tableau of beastly beauty — grand quarters of beef carcasses lined with yellow, grassy fat, and complete goat, lamb and pig carcasses, stretched out and hanging by their hocks. When we look at them, we see the farms they came from and the hard work that brought them here into our cool room, and we're filled with the responsibility of honouring the lives given up to feed us. We walk into the bustling production room where the butchers wield their knives like graceful, efficient sculptors as they break down whole bodies on the hooks, coax bones smoothly out of their fleshy homes and transform whole muscles into elegant portions. Their actions are at once physical and powerful and delicate and precise. A really good butcher has a surgeon's understanding of physiology, and an artist's imagination, and it's beautiful to see the craft at work.

Apart from the skills required, there's an attitude that comes with whole-body butchery. Our youngest butcher, who took a circuitous route into butchery via a partially completed business degree, is in awe of the quality of the animals with which he works and the farmers who produce them. He says that sometimes the butchers will start to break a body and then just stop to step back and admire it for a moment before continuing on with their work. After visiting some of the farms we represent, he has a growing understanding of the ideas behind regenerative agriculture, and the extraordinary effort and commitment that goes into producing the meat he admires so much. He says he is starting to understand the responsibility that he and his colleagues carry. 'When you see how far these farmers go, what they do and the effort they put in, you can see why the quality of the product is so good. As the butcher and the next link in the production chain, I need to match that effort: not waste anything, cut the meat perfectly and advise the customer as well as possible so that they have the best experience, and we all do justice to the farmer and the animal.'

Another butcher observes, 'I have always felt that every body I work with is a gift.'

These are the kinds of butchers we should all want to be preparing the meat we eat.

Having our meat and eating it too

As we've explained throughout this book, the vast majority of agricultural industries, regardless of the product, run according to a commodity model that has dispensed with the quaint, old-fashioned notion of direct relationships in favour of the benefits of speed and scale. A business like ours is a sort of lunatic outpost, clinging to the romantic idea that connecting consumers and producers creates community, and that this is the critical glue that binds us together and holds us all accountable for the choices we make. If you buy your meat at the supermarket, not only are the animal and the farmer likely to be a mystery, but you also don't have any contact with the person who prepared your meat for you. It's a profoundly anonymous exchange. But, as we see from the recipes and stories of all the people in this book, here and all over the world, there is a growing movement that seeks to negotiate a more equitable and sustainable path between the benefits and the costs of industrialised production — or having our meat and eating it too.

The past 20 years has seen an explosion in the number of farmers' markets across the country, serving customers and farmers who want to meet eye to eye. More and more consumers are choosing to scrutinise the food they're putting into their bodies, and more and more farmers are concluding that the intensive method is a hiding to nothing and so they're exploring different methods that lead to overall ecosystem health. There are wonderful opportunities for everyone at every point in the production and consumption cycle to build greater connections and contribute to a healthier, more sustainable food system. Butchery is no exception.

Change is hard and change is slow, but from little things, big things grow.

What is dry ageing?

'Dry ageing' is the traditional practice of hanging some sections of a carcass with an even fat covering in a temperature- and humidity-controlled environment for up to 6 weeks, or even longer. Dry ageing can only be done with meat that remains on the bone, which is partly why so few butchers do it anymore. During this period, the meat loses moisture, shrinks in against the bone, and the exposed flesh on the surface of the cut sections dries evenly and forms a protective layer — the whole protected by the fat, allowing moisture transfer, but dramatically slowing oxidation.

As the moisture evaporates, the muscle tissue is broken down by naturally occurring enzymes that soften the texture and intensify flavour, resulting in more tender meat with a deeply concentrated flavour that is rich and earthy and has a distinct 'umami' savouriness — umami being the fifth of the taste sensations after salty, sweet, bitter and sour.

While mature meat that's been dry aged is a wonderful product, the process of dry ageing requires a dedicated hanging room, careful temperature control and skilled oversight, and results in significant mass and volume losses. All of this needs to be recouped by charging a higher price, which can be difficult in a marketplace that's accustomed to artificially cheap meat and is unfamiliar with this old-fashioned practice.

Here are the average hang times for our carcasses.

- Veal (6–8 months old): 8–14 days

- Beef (24–36 months or older): 2–6+ weeks

- Lambs (5–10 months old): 5–10 days

- Hogget (sheep with two permanent teeth, generally 12–24 months old): 2–3 weeks

- Mutton (sheep with at least four permanent teeth, generally 2 years old or more): 2–6 weeks

- Goats (5–10 months old): 8–14 days

- Suckling pigs (12–18 kg, aged 7–10 weeks): less than 1 week

- Weaner pigs (15–30 kg, aged 8–16 weeks): less than 1 week

- Porker pigs (50–70 kg, aged 20–26 weeks): 5–10 days

There are only a few whole-animal butcheries left in Australia and we're fast losing the skills required to artfully break down a whole body and turn it into the myriad cuts and products it can yield.

Jack Harrington tucks into a spit-roasted rib from a New Horizon Australian White lamb, from Cumnock, NSW.

6.
Delicious on the inside

We are what our food eats

It may require a bit more work and you may eat a little less, but there are ways to eat sustainably produced, ethically raised meat on a budget. The extra effort is well worth the huge benefits in health and nutrition — let alone all the new things you learn when you're more connected to the sources of your food.

Eating is a very intimate act. After all, there aren't many things we do in public (or private) that involve putting foreign objects inside our bodies. In most of these situations we're pretty selective about what and who we choose to allow in.

We do our research, check the risks, make informed choices and trust our instincts. But when it comes to eating, we routinely suspend critical scrutiny, often lavishing our selection of white goods with more attention than we give to the animals or plants we're about to absorb into our own bodies. We rarely actually know where our food comes from, who grew it, how it was grown, or what additives it might contain — from a nauseating smorgasbord of more than 6000 different concoctions, as Joanna Blythman chillingly reveals in her book *Swallow This*, her exposé of the invisible laboratories behind the hugely profitable and secretive processed food industry. It's also likely that more people can decipher ancient Egyptian hieroglyphics than can decode the ingredient lists on most processed-food product labels.

Without an understanding of provenance or production, the only tools available to determine the value of our food are the blunt metrics of cost, aesthetics, ease and convenience. All of which are important and valid, but they only make up half the picture. As we discussed in Chapter 3, the decline in the number of people involved in growing and processing food means that many of us have little understanding of the traditional skills required to feed and care for ourselves and our communities, or the nuanced understanding of natural systems that comes with the hard work of growing food, closely observing nature and transforming a natural product into human food and not wasting a thing.

Left: *Sommerlad heritage chicks tucking into their custom-made grower feed at Grassland Poultry, NSW.*

Unsurprisingly, the combination of our carelessness about food and the increasing opacity in the food path from producer to consumer means that in affluent Western cultures many of us are spending a lot less time than ever before in the preparation and cooking of food. On the surface, this appears to be a perfectly rational response to the increased efficiencies in mechanised food production — fewer people produce more food, more reliably, so that the rest of us can concentrate on doing other things that increase productivity and benefit the community at large. But, despite the fact that we've willingly traded connection and knowledge for cheapness and convenience, there are a growing number of hidden costs that are starting to bite.

The tsunami of diet-related health problems we're grappling with (diabetes is the leading cause of blindness in working-age Australian adults) and the environmental impacts of intensive agriculture are tangible proof that we need to review our attitudes to food. But the dissociation and lack of connection from food also seems to trigger an unresolved need that produces a fascinating social response. There's no other way to explain the bizarre contradictions in our behaviour. On one hand, there's this sharp decline in the time we spend making and cooking food and the importance we attach to the traditional understanding that food is medicine. But on the other hand, we've become utterly obsessed with the idea of food.

Food bloggers and celebrity chefs multiply and erupt from every screen and it's considered quite normal to interrupt a meal and spend as much time posting about it as you do eating it. Faddish diets emerge and fade with stupefying speed, there are thousands of recipes and cooking apps online, cookbooks defy the trend and sell better than any other genre, food films and television series proliferate, and urban streets are choked with meal-delivery-service couriers shunting thousands of meals from restaurants to the homes of people choosing to eat lukewarm, soggy food rather than make a simple meal from scratch. The American journalist and food writer Michael Pollan was so struck by the contradiction between the attention we pay to food and the time we spend cooking that he wrote a very successful book called *Cooked* about his own journey to put aside his devices and reclaim the skill of cooking. Predictably, it was also made into a hugely popular television series, so whether or not it encouraged more people to turn off their devices and head into the kitchen or just gave them more screen food-fodder is debatable.

It seems that the more we obsess over and objectify our food, the less we actually engage with it directly and the more powerless we become. We're not suggesting that we should all give up Netflix and move to a kibbutz, but if we're not armed with knowledge, we're easy pickings for the marketers, diet pushers and zealots wanting to manipulate us. In addition, our concern about the impacts of agricultural malpractice on climate change and our growing willingness to consider making different, more environmentally sustainable

'Balancing ethical and economic demands can be a nail-bitingly difficult tightrope to walk.'

purchasing decisions makes us even more vulnerable. We desperately want to do the right thing, but we're not well enough informed to filter through the shouting claims. Organic, seasonal, local, grass-fed, hand-sourced, hand-reared, chemical-free, fair trade, sustainable, ethical, pastured, free range, biodynamic, washed in rainwater and packaged in angel eyelashes? Sure, whatever you want. But how do you check that any of it is true?

Governments legislate on our behalf with little scrutiny, deciding what we do and don't need to know about our food and the way it's produced. Food technologies are being developed with such speed that they're outpacing our capacity to test them, and regulators can't keep up. We cower guiltily as legions of skeletal, bouncing wellness experts with fabulous abs and blindingly white teeth harangue us about how we should live and what diet we should follow, when what we really need to do is reconnect with our instinctive ability to self-medicate and stay healthy by eating a balanced diet of varied, unprocessed, locally sourced, seasonal and chemical-free foods. Toss in regular exercise (surprise), laugh as much as possible and forgive ourselves our trespasses (such as the occasional over-indulgence in good chocolate or gin).

Given all this confusion, it's no wonder that some of us scuttle to the edges and take cover at one or other end of the spectrum — either putting our heads in the sand and dismissing all the concerns as rabid fear-mongering, or latching on to the seductive — but deceptive — idea that meat is the problem and that, simply by opting out of eating meat, we're taking positive action for a better planet. If only it were that simple!

Of course, if you don't eat meat, you're not personally complicit in the death of animals. But neither does your choice prevent others eating intensively produced meat or in any way curb the abuses perpetrated by the intensive livestock industry. The only way to do that in a free market system is to offer consumers a compelling alternative — more modest numbers of animals raised in a sustainable, compassionate and ecologically beneficial system. But the only way that alternative is going to flourish is if consumers vote for it at the checkout. If you opt out, you have no impact. Nor are the problems with intensive food production systems restricted to meat — intensive plant agriculture is riddled with unacceptable practices that have profound environmental impacts. So, if you're going to reject intensively produced meat, then the same discretion should be applied to the plant foods you consume. Which, in a country like Australia, raises the tricky question of land use. An omnivorous diet that includes a balance of plants and animal products is viable in most landscapes because animals can be raised on land that isn't fit for crops. But, in the driest inhabited continent in the world with a very low proportion of arable land, if more of us move to a vegetarian diet, how are we going to increase our local, sustainably managed plant food industry to match demand? Is it acceptable to destroy habitats and clear land for crops?

But most of us don't lurch to one side or another. We take a middle path, trotting along confidently and feeling virtuous about some of the choices we make, and faltering and feeling unsure about others. We all want to do the right thing, but balancing ethical and economic demands can be a nail-bitingly difficult tightrope to walk.

The cost of food in affluent Western countries has dropped significantly over the past 50 years. In Australia, we spend only about 10 per cent of our income on food, which makes us around the ninth lowest food-spending country in the world — it's telling that half of that is spent on meals cooked outside the home. Yet while we romp to the supermarket for our cheap goods, there's a growing sense of discomfort that things may not be what they seem. As the impacts of climate change become more apparent, the idea that there may be a cause and effect relationship between the way we manage agriculture, water, energy and urban planning is crystallising for more and more of us. Hopefully, we won't take ourselves to the brink of disaster before we start actively connecting the dots and implementing more holistic strategies for mitigating climate change. But, at this point in the story, our food purchasing decisions are still simply based on advertising campaigns, the behavioural norms of our peers and what a product costs, looks and tastes like. We've become infantilised, and it is time to rouse ourselves from our torpor and take back control over our food choices.

But navigating your way through the minefield of claims and counter-claims about food production to make the right choice is fraught with difficulty and, in this landscape, meat is arguably the most controversial and misunderstood ingredient of all. As we've discovered in running our butchery, when it comes to eating meat, people's approaches and patterns of consumption vary and fluctuate for all sorts of reasons.

Our customers include lifelong omnivores, carnivores who only eat meat, carnivores who only eat raw meat, vegetarians feeding meat to their families

Right: At Grassland Poultry, the Sommerlad heritage chickens are fed whole grains that hold greater nutritional value than the standard chicken diet of cracked or milled grain. Processing whole grains stimulates the entire digestive system and results in a stronger, healthier bird. Unlike conventional poultry that are vaccinated and given medicated feed, Sommerlad chickens are entirely free of medication. Find out more about Grassland Poultry and Sommerlad chickens on page 64.

'Genuine deliciousness is predetermined before the product arrives in our hands.'

or pets, and former vegetarians and vegans who, for any number of reasons, have decided to start eating meat again. Some people eat meat daily, some weekly, and some once a month. Some are motivated by health issues and are looking for pure, clean food to treat ailments from anorexia and autism to allergies, food intolerances and chronic inflammatory diseases, many of which are increasingly attributed to the build-up of chemicals in the intensive food production system. Others are alarmed by the growing connections between intensive agriculture and climate change, and are determined to seek out and support more benign food systems. Some are moved by animal welfare and ethical concerns, and others are simply chasing the quality delivered by healthy ecosystems. The reasons people seek out meat and products from animals raised on farms that operate outside the intensive food system are as varied as the cuts that a beef carcass yields.

But is it delicious?

We'd argue that meat from these farms is incomparably more full-flavoured, satiating and just downright delicious than the meat that comes out of the intensive system.

If you're eating meat from a healthy animal, you'll find yourself satiated with less. The feeling of satiety is our body's way of telling us when it's received enough of the chemical compounds to meet our needs: 'Stop eating now, we're all stocked up.' In fact, as the animal behaviourist Fred Provenza explains in his fascinating book *Nourishment: What animals can teach us about rediscovering our nutritional wisdom*, when humans eat a broad variety of plants or animals that are themselves healthy and nutritionally well-balanced and in forms that aren't highly processed, we find ourselves satiated after eating comparatively small quantities. In addition, the greater the variety of healthy foods, the greater the smorgasbord of naturally occurring beneficial chemical compounds your body has to choose from to satisfy its needs.

But if the food we're eating is intrinsically lacking or compromised, then our hypothalamus tells us to keep eating — either because the triggers that tell us to stop aren't present in the food, or because it takes a larger quantity to achieve the levels of chemicals our body needs. As Provenza explains:

> 'The presence of phytochemicals in whole foods limits how much of any one food we can eat. That enhances health through nutrition by exposing a body to a wide array of phytochemicals, thus enabling cells to pick and choose from a variety of compounds. With energy-dense processed foods, the appetite-stimulating effects of variety aren't offset by the appetite-moderating effects of phytochemicals.'

This is a major factor in the obesity epidemic and associated diseases that are rife in affluent Western countries.

Despite the fact that we all bandy the word 'delicious' about as though there's some sort of common definition, flavour is entirely subjective and based on familiarity. If you are used to commodity yearling beef (15–20 months old) that has been 'finished' on a grain ration in a feedlot, you might find dry-aged beef from a 3-year-old pasture-fed and finished steer confrontingly rich and 'beefy'. This becomes quite a challenge when the national palate has grown accustomed to the flavour of intensively produced meat, ceases to recognise or demand something better and more nutritious, and loses the skill to prepare it properly.

When something is referred to as delicious, what we're really talking about is the appeal of the five tastes and the way we conjure those up when we cook. These are the cues that food technologists use so successfully when they develop the artificial food additives that are present in otherwise bland or non-shelf-stable processed foods and it's surprisingly easy to tweak our taste buds without us even knowing it's happening. Many retail butchers, for example, rely heavily on pre-prepared, commercial marinades to add more flavour to intensively produced meat that is intrinsically bland. But while additives or a skilled cook can turn the blandest produce into something appetising, it takes a lot of work and alchemy for that to happen.

To us, deliciousness isn't achieved by simply adding something to the core ingredients. In fact, we'd say that genuine deliciousness is something that is predetermined before the product arrives in our hands. The work to make our meat 'delicious' started way back at the beginning of the story, with the slow and steady fostering of the healthy farm ecosystem into which the animal that gave us the meat was born. When all the elements of that environment, from the tiniest to the largest creatures, sang together in a great, complex daily chorus of life and death, much of which we humans are only now just starting to understand, then the potential for producing real deliciousness was present. So when a butcher or a cook is presented with meat that is sung into deliciousness in this way, the real challenge isn't what to do to it — but rather what not to do to it, so that you are amplifying rather than masking its intrinsic deliciousness!

This is good news for those of us who are a bit tentative in the kitchen. Start with skilfully handled and butchered meat from healthy animals that are genetically strong, that have been given free range to express instinctive behaviours, and have had access to a diverse and complex diet. Then, considering which part of the animal it comes from and whether it requires slow or fast cooking, do as little as possible to it so you don't get in the way of the quality. Pour yourself a glass of your favourite tipple, put on some music and let the meat do the work. For the fancy-pants chefs among us, working with flavour-rich, nutrient-dense meat is also a delight, because a deft and clever hand can take really good produce to culinary heights that are very hard to reach if you're starting with a less-flavoursome product.

A lot has been written about the unsustainable cost of cheap meat by people much more knowledgeable than us (see Further reading on page 248 for some of them). We make no bones about where we sit regarding the profound problems with the commodity meat industry, and we've staked our livelihoods on promoting regenerative agriculture as a way to build a more compassionate, resilient and sustainable food production landscape. To us and many of our customers, seeking out and eating food from healthy systems is a matter of life and death. But we're not naive about the stumbling blocks consumers face when they're considering changing their behaviour.

Voting for more sustainable food production systems doesn't have to cost you an arm and a leg, and is within the reach of most of us. A glass of water is

'This is where whole-body, traditional cooking skills that we've let slip come back into play.'

cheaper and better for you than the 39 grams of sugar in a can of Coca-Cola, and 500 grams of pasture-raised minced beef (containing nothing but beef) is the same price as a well-known fast-food burger (containing a battlefield of synthetic preservatives, emulsifiers, antioxidants, thickener, colours, flavours, acidity regulators, sugar and dehydrated onion). It may require a bit more work to source and prepare, and it may mean you eat a little less, but there are ways to eat sustainably produced, ethically raised meat on a budget, and the extra effort is well worth the huge benefits in health and nutrition — let alone all the new things you learn when you're more connected to the sources of your food. This is where the whole-body approach and those traditional cooking skills that we've let slip over the last few generations come back into play.

Half a kilogram of minced pasture-fed and finished beef with a little offal mixed through and a few hours of slow cooking will make a rich, super-healthy meat sauce with a hearty boost of vitamin B (see page 183). A kilogram of humble beef chuck makes a great pot roast that gives and gives — dinner with loads of veg, sliced on sandwiches for lunch, and shredded through a mixed salad for a third meal (see page 184). Those bones from your roast chook will make a fabulous stock for a soup or a mushroom risotto, giving you one and a half meals for the price of one — and don't forget to skim some of the fat off while you're roasting to use later for frying potatoes, or anything really (see page 204). Those pig's ears you were going to give the dog? Marinate and braise them, then crumb and fry and use them in a banh mi (see page 205).

What follows here is a selection of recipes drawn from all corners of our extended community, people who bring their unique perspective on food and cooking to bear on both the humblest and most luxurious of ingredients. We hope that in trying these recipes, or just using them as a starting point for your own culinary creativity, that you not only strengthen the connections between you and those you feed, but also with those who labour to provide you with the ingredients worthy of your care, love and skill.

Recipes for conscientious carnivory from friends of Feather and Bone.

These recipes come from our community, the people with whom we interact at every turn in our business. Chefs, butchers, farmers, activists and domestic cooks from all walks of life — a democratic stew of people, united by a love of good food and a determination to make compassionate food choices that support a healthier planet. Their recipes are as diverse and individual as they are and cover all parts of the animal, ranging from simple to complex.

Start with rendering fats and simmering broth, then try Norwegian shanks, South Indian goat fry, pig's ear banh mi or vitello lingua tonnato and finish with a whole roasted Greek lamb on the spit. There's something here for everyone.

Let's eat

Laura's rendered animal fats, page 144.

7.
I can
do that

Short and fat(s)

Simple recipes from schnitzel,
salads, pasta sauce and roasts,
to rendered fat and pâtés. All on
the table in under 2½ hours.

Brent's bacon jam

'I began a career as a pastry chef when I came here from New Zealand in 2003. Over time, I've moved away from the overly decorative and fanciful style of modern patisserie and into a more simple and natural style of cooking. A knowledge of good techniques and the traditions of our food can take you a lot further than the latest trends ever will.

This is a great condiment to add to a burger, chicken schnitzel or sausage sizzle, but it is just as satisfying on its own with fresh crusty bread, and a cold beer, of course. Red onions, red wine and red wine vinegar give a slightly fruity flavour. Brown onions, black coffee and malt vinegar give a dark, almost bitter caramel note. Take your pick as to which version you prefer.'

Brent Templeton, chef

———

Makes: about 800 g (3 cups) | Preparation time: 10 minutes | Cooking time: 50 minutes

2 tablespoons olive oil
500 g (1 lb 2 oz) smoked bacon rashers,
 very thinly sliced
2 garlic cloves, crushed
100 g (3½ oz/½ cup lightly packed)
 soft brown sugar

Fruity jam

500 g (1 lb 2 oz/2¾ cups) red onions,
 thinly sliced
125 ml (4 fl oz/½ cup) red wine
1½ tablespoons red wine vinegar

Caramel jam

500 g (1 lb 2 oz/2¾ cups) brown onions,
 thinly sliced
125 ml (4 fl oz/½ cup) black coffee
1½ tablespoons malt vinegar

Heat olive oil in a large frying pan over medium heat, add bacon and fry, stirring occasionally, for 5–10 minutes until crisp and golden and the fat has rendered. Remove with a slotted spoon and drain on paper towel.

Add onion to the bacon fat (red for fruity; brown for caramel) and cook over low heat, stirring occasionally, for about 15 minutes, or until starting to caramelise. Add garlic and cook, stirring occasionally, for another 5–10 minutes until soft.

Return bacon to pan and stir in sugar. Add red wine and red wine vinegar for the fruity version, or coffee and malt vinegar for the caramel version, then season to taste with salt and freshly ground black pepper. Reduce heat to low and cook, stirring constantly to make sure it doesn't catch on the pan, for about 15 minutes or until it becomes sticky and jammy. Bacon jam will keep, refrigerated, for up to a month.

Brendan's lamb rump with green sauce

'This makes a regular appearance at home. It's equally good with goat or kid, which tends to give a bigger portion. If you don't have the number or appetite for a leg of lamb, this is a quick and easy way to get your protein fix, and a slice or two is enough to balance all those lovely veg you'll be roasting at the same time. I mainly use parsley in the green sauce, but mint, basil or rocket can make an appearance too. I like to serve this with roasted cauliflower topped with tahini and pine nuts, or a salad of grilled zucchini with feta and mint.'

Brendan Hilferty, winemaker and retail customer

———

Feeds: 2–4 | Preparation time: 10 minutes | Cooking time: 30 minutes

1 tablespoon olive oil
500–700 g (1 lb 2 oz–1 lb 9 oz) whole
   lamb or goat rump
2 dill pickles, finely chopped
1 teaspoon capers, rinsed and
   finely chopped
3 spring onions (scallions), finely chopped
1 handful flat-leaf parsley leaves,
   finely chopped
1 teaspoon Dijon mustard
2 teaspoons red wine vinegar
100 ml (3½ fl oz) extra-virgin olive oil,
   plus extra as needed

Preheat oven to 190°C (375°F). Heat olive oil in an ovenproof frying pan over high heat. Season lamb rumps with salt and freshly ground black pepper and cook, turning, for 3–5 minutes until browned on all sides. Transfer pan to oven and roast for 20–25 minutes for medium–rare or until cooked to your liking. Remove lamb and rest for 5 minutes.

Meanwhile, combine pickle, capers, spring onion, parsley, mustard, vinegar and extra-virgin olive oil in a bowl. Add more olive oil to adjust the thickness of the sauce to your liking. Season with salt and freshly ground black pepper.

Slice lamb across the grain, and pour over the juices that have collected as it rested. Serve with green sauce and whatever side you like.

Kathryn's stuffed Sommerlad chook with apple, pine nuts and bacon

'Michael and I stuff our roast chickens because that's what our parents did and, in our minds, it was how you treated the whole occasion with more care. Shoving it in the oven without seasoning seemed to mean you didn't care as much. Also, we had a heap of kids (10) who loved it and when they started working on the farm, their appetites were huge and the stuffing made the meal go even further. Maybe that's why our parents did it too? It wasn't long before I realised that a lot of modern, fancy-pants chefs and those who ate at their restaurants found it a bit old-fashioned. Regardless, we think it's really delicious.'

Kathryn Sommerlad, producer

Feeds: 6, depending on the size of the chook | Preparation time: 15 minutes
Cooking time: 1½ hours | Special equipment: Kitchen string

1 whole Sommerlad chicken (about 2 kg)

Stuffing

275 g (9¾ oz/2½ cups) fresh
  breadcrumbs
2–3 French shallots, sliced
2 tablespoons chopped flat-leaf parsley
2 teaspoons mixed dried or fresh
  green herbs
1–2 rashers belly bacon, finely chopped
1 small apple, peeled and finely chopped
40 g (1½ oz/¼ cup) pine nuts
3 tablespoons olive oil, plus extra to drizzle
1 beaten egg (optional)

Preheat oven to 170°C (325°F) — Sommerlad chooks grow more slowly than conventional white Cobb or Ross chooks, so low and slow is the best way to go.

Combine stuffing ingredients, except the olive oil, in a bowl, and season to taste with salt and freshly ground black pepper. Add just enough olive oil to bring everything together. If you prefer a firmer stuffing add the egg. Spoon stuffing into the cavity, pressing in lightly as you go. Tie the legs together with kitchen string and tuck the wings under. Rub the whole chook with olive oil and season generously with salt and freshly ground black pepper.

Roast for 1½ hours or until golden and the juices run clear when a thigh is pierced with a skewer. Cooking time will vary depending on the size of the bird. Remove from oven, cover loosely with foil and allow the meat to rest for 10 minutes before serving. Make sure you save the carcass to make a delicious chicken stock.

Topher's Tex-Mex skirt tortillas with sour cream and salsa

'I arrived in Australia from Texas in 2009 to be with my now wife. I started making beer professionally in 2013 and along the way became interested in native fermentations and making beer with a sense of place. In 2016, I brought together lessons learned across the world, adapted them and started Wildflower Brewing & Blending, focusing on making wild-fermented beer using regional ingredients.

I cook Tex-Mex food at home a lot and love this dish because it can feed a crowd. You can serve the steak with tortillas, sour cream, guacamole and a slice of lime or on a bed of lettuce and seasonal roasted vegies. Skirt steak is also generally pretty cheap.'

Topher Boehm, brewer and retail customer

———

Feeds: 8 | Preparation time: 10 minutes, plus marinating | Cooking time: 10 minutes

Finely grated zest and juice of 1 orange

Finely grated zest and juice of 2 lemons or the flesh of 2 finger limes

160 g (5¾ oz/1 cup) finely chopped pineapple or 3 tablespoons pineapple juice

3 tablespoons dry white wine

3 tablespoons soy sauce

2–3 dried chillies (I like mixing chili de arbol with guajillo and ancho chillies, available from select grocers and online)

1 tablespoon coarsely ground black pepper

1 garlic clove, crushed

1 kg (2 lb 4 oz) skirt steak, trimmed of membrane and excess fat

Tortillas, sour cream, fresh salsa, guacamole and lime wedges, to serve

Mix up all the ingredients, except the steak, with a splash of water in a large bowl. Add steaks, refrigerate, and let them have a bath in the liquid for 1–2 hours.

Drain the marinade and cook steaks, turning once, over hot coals (or under a grill, or on a gas barbecue on high heat) for 8–10 minutes, until medium–rare (but no longer or they'll be tough). Skirt needs to be seared at high heat so it doesn't stew and toughen.

Remove from heat, rest for about 10 minutes, then slice meat against the grain into long strips about the width of your pinkie finger.

Serve steak with tortillas, sour cream, fresh salsa, guacamole and lime wedges.

Feather and Bone's lamb long things (kofta) with yoghurt sauce

When Feather and Bone was in its infancy and we were desperate for a base to work from, Grant found Tanta Meats, owned by Egyptian-Australian butcher Nabil Oussa. He kindly agreed to rent us some space and it was our home for the next three years. He's a Coptic Christian, fasts on Fridays and eschews meat for Lent. As a committed part-time vegetarian, he also makes the most wonderful falafel, tossing armfuls of fragrant fresh herbs into a huge mixing machine. On one of these falafel days, with the heady, spicy aromatics heavy in the air, Nabil noticed Grant making these hand-rolled sausages, and casually suggested going easy on the cumin and upping the cinnamon to avoid bitterness. And it's true: the secret here is equal parts cinnamon and cumin. Adding some chilli flakes works well, but please don't mess with the proportions of these two spices. If you are cooking the sausages within 24 hours, finely chopped onion is a good addition, but it doesn't keep well, so omit if you are planning on storing or freezing the mix for a few days.

Feeds: 4–6 | Preparation time: 20 minutes, plus chilling | Cooking time: 10 minutes

1 kg (2 lb 4 oz) minced (ground) lamb shoulder (ideally medium coarseness, with 20 per cent fat)
2 teaspoons salt
½ teaspoon ground cumin
½ teaspoon freshly ground black pepper
½ teaspoon ground cinnamon
1 garlic clove, crushed
1 handful flat-leaf parsley leaves, finely chopped
1 handful coriander (cilantro) leaves and stems, finely chopped
1 tablespoon olive oil
Bitter leaves dressed with vinaigrette, to serve
Lemon wedges, to serve

Yoghurt sauce
130 g (4½ oz/½ cup) natural yoghurt
1 teaspoon ground cumin
2 teaspoons olive oil
1 teaspoon salt
1 tablespoon finely chopped mint

Combine lamb, salt, spices, garlic and herbs in a non-reactive bowl and mix well by hand, to activate the proteins and help the mixture stick together. At this point you can refrigerate the lamb mixture for up to 3 days, or proceed straight to portioning into 100 g (3½ oz) pieces. Gently roll each portion back and forth on a cool bench to obtain a uniform thickness. If you don't have kitchen scales, just do whatever feels right and keep them all a similar size; if you're feeding six people, make them a little smaller so you finish with 12 pieces. Refrigerate for 15 minutes to firm up.

Meanwhile, combine all yoghurt sauce ingredients in a bowl. Loosen with just enough water to allow the sauce to be poured.

Bring the 'long things' to room temperature. Heat olive oil in a frying pan over medium–high heat and fry them, turning, for 5–10 minutes, or until nicely browned with a hint of scorch on the outside and still gently pink in the centre. (Alternatively, rub them with oil and grill over a charcoal fire.)

Serve hot on a bitter leaf salad accompanied with lemon wedges and yoghurt sauce.

Angie's anticuchos

'I first tried this when I was travelling in Peru and it's the most popular of the delicious street foods made with grilled or barbecued meat. The real name for this dish is Anticuchos de Corazón (beef heart skewers) and it's very easy to make. I'm a passionate supporter of sustainable food practices, an avid cook and lover of all things food, particularly those less popular, "secondary" cuts of meat. When I'm not cooking or eating I'm developing ways to share skills and recipes with others. This recipe is a quick and easy way to turn an overlooked ingredient into something everyone finds delicious. Try my Humble pie recipe on page 214, which also brings the joys of frequently overlooked cuts to the table.'

Angie Prendergast-Sceats, chef and educator

──────

Feeds: 4 | Preparation time: 15 minutes, plus soaking and marinating | Cooking time: 3 minutes
Special equipment: Bamboo skewers soaked in hot water for 30 minutes

500 g (1 lb 2 oz) beef or veal heart, trimmed (ask your butcher to do this) and cut into 2.5–3 cm (1–1¼ in) pieces
200 ml (7 fl oz) extra-virgin olive oil
125 ml (4 fl oz/½ cup) red wine vinegar
6 garlic cloves, crushed
2 long red chillies, coarsely chopped
2 teaspoons chipotle in adobo sauce
3 teaspoons ground cumin
3 teaspoons paprika
1 teaspoon dried chilli flakes
1 small handful finely chopped coriander (cilantro) and parsley leaves

Combine all ingredients with 2 teaspoons salt and 1 teaspoon freshly ground black pepper in a bowl and toss to combine. Refrigerate for 30 minutes to 1 hour to marinate.

Preheat a barbecue to high, thread 3 pieces of heart onto each skewer until all the heart has been used. Grill, turning occasionally, for 2–3 minutes until golden and cooked through. Be careful not to overcook skewers as heart will become tough.

Gaby's arroz tapado

'There are lots of different cultural influences in my food. I live in Sydney, but I was born and raised in Lima, Peru, to my Peruvian father and Japanese mother. My Japanese grandmother had a ravioli business in Lima. I remember watching cooking shows with her when I was little, and she influenced me to be adventurous with food. I'm now an Accredited Practising Dietitian and Krav Maga instructor with a strong interest in sports nutrition. Arroz tapado (literally 'covered rice') is a comforting classic with an additional nutritional charge.'

Gaby Moran, retail customer

Feeds: 4–6 | Preparation time: 15 minutes | Cooking time: 45 minutes

600 g (1 lb 5 oz) minced beef (or 500 g beef mince enriched with 100 g minced organ meats such as heart and/or liver)
2 tablespoons ghee or olive oil
3 garlic cloves, finely chopped
1 large red onion, finely chopped
250 ml (9 fl oz/1 cup) beef/vegetable stock
1 tablespoon ají amarillo paste (available online or from South American grocers, or substitute adobo sauce)
½ teaspoon ground chilli
45 g (1½ oz/¼ cup) raisins
35 g (1¼ oz/¼ cup) black olives, quartered
1 egg, hard-boiled

Rice

1 tablespoon ghee or olive oil
4 garlic cloves, crushed
440 g (15½ oz/2 cups) medium-grain white rice

To make the rice, heat ghee or olive oil in a saucepan over medium–low heat. Add garlic, sauté for 2–3 minutes until softened but not browned, then add rice and stir to coat. Add 750 ml (26 fl oz/ 3 cups) water and 1 teaspoon salt, cover with a lid, bring to the boil, then reduce to a simmer. Cook for 20 minutes or until all the water has been absorbed. Meanwhile, bring beef to room temperature.

Heat ghee or olive oil over medium–high heat in a large frying pan. Add beef, season with salt, and cook, stirring and breaking mince up with a wooden spoon, for 5–10 minutes until browned.

Transfer beef to a bowl, reduce heat to low, then add garlic and onion and 2 tablespoons stock to deglaze, scraping base of pan. Increase heat to medium, add chilli paste and ground chilli, and simmer, stirring occasionally, for 10 minutes or until slightly reduced. Add beef and remaining stock, then simmer for 5 minutes or until flavours combine and liquid is slightly reduced. Season to taste with salt and freshly ground black pepper, then add raisins and olives and stir to heat through.

Cut egg into as many wedges as people you'll be feeding.

To assemble, spread a layer of rice in the base of a small bowl (a dessert bowl is ideal), and press it with the back of a spoon. Place an egg wedge in the middle, spread a layer of filling on top and cover with another layer of rice, pressing it down. Place a plate on top of the bowl and invert carefully. Repeat with as many bowls as people you're feeding. Serve with a salad of your choice.

O Tama's buffalo yoghurt mango lassi with pistachio and cardamom

'I have had the pleasure of using Feather and Bone produce in restaurants I have worked in for over 10 years. Since we opened Lankan Filling Station, they have been our sole supplier of meat, we use their eggs and they also provide me with one of the few buffalo yoghurts available in Australia. The yoghurt is always on our dessert menu served simply with kithul, a Sri Lankan palm-sugar treacle, a dish that is a Sri Lankan staple. We also use the yoghurt in our lassi — traditionally an Indian drink, it's made with fruit or it comes as a sweet or salty version seasoned with spices. Our version is a super-simple recipe and combines both these ideas, always a fruit, changing with the seasons and topped with spiced pistachio crumb.'

O Tama Carey, chef

———

Makes: 2 | Preparation time: 5 minutes | Cooking time: 10 minutes

Mango lassi
300 g (10½ oz) buffalo yoghurt (from select grocers and butchers)
300 g (10½ oz) coarsely chopped ripe mango (or other seasonal fruit)
2 tablespoons condensed milk
360 g ice

Pistachio crumb
1½ tablespoons pistachio nut kernels
A tiny pinch of ground cardamom
A tiny pinch of salt flakes

Preheat oven to 150°C (300°F). To make pistachio crumb, spread pistachios on a baking tray and roast, tossing once or twice, for 8 minutes or until light golden. Transfer to a mortar with cardamom and salt, and coarsely grind with a pestle.

Place yoghurt, mango, condensed milk and ice into a blender and blend until smooth.

Pour lassi into tall glasses and sprinkle with pistachio crumb to serve.

Lorenzo's pork fat butter with rosemary and salt

We first met Lorenzo at the 2012 Melbourne Food and Wine Festival when we attended an event with him and his mentor and family friend, the renowned Italian butcher Dario Cecchini. Lorenzo fell for Australia and we fell for Lorenzo so we lured him up to Feather and Bone to work in our team. But six months later, on the brink of us sponsoring him, Lorenzo fell in love again, this time with a Finnish backpacker who led him off to Finland, where he eventually embarked on a new career in International Business and Logistics and lived happily ever after with his new wife. Fortunately, he left us with the recipe for the delicious pork fat butter that he learned at Dario's Macelleria Cecchini.

Lorenzo Ciatti, butcher and former staffer

———

Makes: 250 g | Preparation time: 20 minutes

200 g (7 oz) pork back fat, finely ground
   (if possible, ask your butcher to grind it
   twice, or chop it finely with a sharp knife
   so it's easy to knead)
25 g (1 oz) rosemary leaves,
   very finely chopped
Finely ground sea salt, to taste
½ teaspoon red wine vinegar
Fresh crusty bread, to serve

Place ground pork fat in a bowl and sprinkle it with rosemary, salt and freshly ground black pepper to taste. Add a splash of vinegar, adjusting to taste — the vinegar is for cutting the richness of the fat, but too much will ruin the balance of flavours.

Mix ingredients together with your hands until they're sticking together, then tip contents onto a clean, flat surface (a kitchen bench made of stone is ideal). Knead the mixture with the palm of your hand as if you were kneading dough, folding it over and kneading again until the mixture is fully combined.

Scrape it all up, put it into a bowl and spread it liberally on fresh, crusty bread. It will keep refrigerated for a few days, but it's best eaten fresh.

Laura's rendered animal fats

'I started rendering animal fat to use as a substitute for other fats and oils for my daughter with food allergies. Fats from healthy, pasture-raised animals, free ranging in the Aussie sun, are full of readily absorbable nutrition and energy for her. I use the fat around the kidney as it has a pure taste. Animal fats are very stable at high heats; they can be added to soups, stews, and used for baking or frying, and even whipped and enjoyed like butter. A couple of years ago I discovered that goat kidney fat is a magnificent white fat and great for rendering, although any variety of animal fat works perfectly and they each have their own amazing nutrient profiles. My daughter's favourite part of rendering fat is hanging around to snack on the 'cracklings' that are left behind.

This recipe can be made with any amount of fat — just adjust the size of the sauce-pan as necessary. The yield will be about 80 per cent of the original quantity.'

Laura Jarvis, retail customer

_____

Makes: About 80 per cent of what you start with | Preparation time: 5 minutes
Cooking time: 30–40 minutes | Special equipment: muslin (cheesecloth)

Trimmed animal fat, chilled in the freezer for 1 hour

Cut fat into 1 cm (½ in) dice, transfer to a cold saucepan and place over low–medium heat. Cook, stirring occasionally, for 30–40 minutes or until fat has turned to liquid with small pieces of crackling floating in it.

Remove cracklings with a slotted spoon and discard (or feed them to your kids). Strain fat into jars through a fine sieve lined with muslin (cheesecloth). Cool to room temperature, then store in the fridge until ready to use. Rendered fat will keep refrigerated for up to 6–8 weeks, or frozen for up to a year.

Try using these fats for Bryan's bombproof chicken sofrito on page 148, or Julian's Wiener schnitzel on page 158. You could also fry or roast your favourite vegetables with it, or lather it on toast.

Katie's orange blossom Moroccan-spiced chicken

'I started my food career in the late 1970s, as a cadet journalist in the test kitchen of *Woman's Day* magazine, under the excellent guidance of cooking legend Margaret Fulton. I went on to have a catering business in the 1980s, and after a long stint as a magazine food editor I now make Katie Swift Cordials for cafes, restaurants and bars. I am very proud to have my cordial at Feather and Bone. I believe it is imperative to know where one's meat has come from, and that it has been sustainably produced and the animal humanely treated. This chicken recipe is based on one published by Karen Martini about a decade or so ago. I love all the flavours and it has become a strong favourite at family lunches.'

Katie Swift, retail customer and producer

———

Feeds: 4–6 | Preparation time: 10 minutes | Cooking time: 1½ hours

80 g (2¾ oz/½ cup) raw almonds
1 large (about 2 kg/4 lb oz) pasture-raised chicken
3 tablespoons olive oil
1–2 garlic cloves, crushed
1 tablespoon Herbie's Spices ras el hanout or other high-quality Moroccan spice blend
1 tablespoon orange blossom water
1 tablespoon pomegranate molasses
Finely grated zest and juice of 1 lemon
2 handfuls coriander (cilantro) leaves, coarsely chopped
2 tablespoons Bitton Orange Jelly, or your favourite bitter orange marmalade
75 g (2½ oz/½ cup) currants
50 g (1¾ oz/1 cup firmly packed) coarsely chopped mint
Seeds of 1 pomegranate
75 g (2½ oz) coarsely chopped preserved lemon rind

Preheat oven to 180°C (350°F). Place almonds on a baking tray and toast for 5 minutes, or until lightly golden. Remove from oven and coarsely chop.

Dry chicken inside and out with paper towel, and place on a wire rack set in a roasting tin. Combine olive oil, garlic, ras el hanout, orange blossom water, pomegranate molasses, lemon zest, half the lemon juice and half the coriander.

Rub chicken all over with oil and spice mix, place in oven and roast, basting twice, for 1 hour–1 hour 15 minutes or until the juices run clear when a thigh is pierced with a skewer. Remove chicken from oven, transfer to a plate to rest, and pour roasting juices into a saucepan.

Add orange jelly to juices in pan, place over medium heat, and cook for 5–10 minutes or until reduced by half. Remove from heat and add remaining lemon juice.

Carve chicken into pieces and arrange on serving platter. Pour orange sauce over chicken, then scatter with almonds, currants, mint, remaining coriander, pomegranate seeds and preserved lemon. Serve with cous cous, brown rice or crispy potatoes and a salad of mixed leaves.

Bryan's bombproof chicken sofrito

'This dish is inspired by Yotam Ottolenghi and Sami Tamimi's chicken sofrito recipe but I've adapted it a bit over time. Sofrito is more of a cooking method than a recipe — it originates from the Spanish verb *sofreír*, which means to lightly fry, and it involves slowly cooking the meat in a pot on the stove for a long time, with only oil and a little liquid. There are lots of ways to cook sofrito but I reckon this recipe is bombproof and I play around with the herbs and spices I use. Here I've used lemon myrtle and pepperberry, but it works with whatever I have to hand.'

Bryan Kiss, producer

———

Feeds: 4–6 | Preparation time: 10 minutes | Cooking time: 1½ hours
Special equipment: A large, shallow, heavy-based saucepan with a lid

1 tablespoon schmaltz (chicken fat) or sunflower oil
1 Sommerlad chicken (about 2 kg), butterflied and quartered
Ground lemon myrtle and pepperberry (available online, or substitute herbs and spices of your choosing), to taste
1 large brown onion, quartered
Sunflower oil, for deep-frying
750 g (1 lb 10 oz) starchy potatoes, peeled and cut into 2 cm (¾ in) dice
1 garlic bulb, broken into cloves

Heat schmaltz or oil in a large frying pan over medium heat. Arrange the pieces of chicken skin-side down in the pan, and sear until golden brown, around 4–5 minutes. Sprinkle thoroughly with lemon myrtle, pepperberry and salt, until fragrant.

Turn the chicken skin-side up and add onion, arranging around the pan to evenly distribute the flavour, before covering with a lid. Reduce heat to as low as it will go and simmer gently for 1 hour. The chicken will release its fat and juices, but keep an eye on it as it cooks — you may need to add a little bit of chicken stock or water if it's drying out or sticking.

Meanwhile, heat 3 cm (1¼ in) oil in a saucepan over medium heat. The oil is hot enough when a piece of potato sizzles immediately when added. Working in batches, add potato and garlic in batches and fry, turning gently, for 5–6 minutes until they start to colour and turn crisp. Remove with a slotted spoon and drain on paper towel. Season to taste with salt.

Once the chicken has been cooking for 1 hour, remove chicken from pan. Add fried potatoes and garlic to pan and toss them in the cooking juices, then return chicken to the pan so it sits on top. Cover with lid and simmer for another 30 minutes until chicken, potatoes and garlic are tender.

Feather and Bone's chicken liver pâté

Back in the day, organ meats were prized and understood to pack a valuable nutritional punch, full of protein and essential vitamins and minerals. Unfortunately, organ meats have fallen out of popular favour and many of us now find them intimidating and mystifying. This is where chicken liver pâté comes in handy, because even the most squeamish among us find a rich, buttery, creamy pâté pretty irresistible. But it pays to get your organs from healthy animals. For example, the liver's main job is to filter and detoxify the blood; excrete bilirubin, cholesterol, hormones and drugs; and metabolise fats, proteins and carbohydrates. The more you know about how the animal was raised, the more able you are to determine whether or not the liver you're about to cook and absorb into your body had to battle against the odds to keep its owner healthy, or if it hummed along nicely within a healthy animal ecosystem.

Makes: 750 g (1 lb 10 oz) | Preparation time: 15 minutes, plus chilling
Cooking time: 20 minutes | Special equipment: A terrine mould

2 brown onions, finely chopped
2 garlic cloves, finely chopped
100 g (3½ oz) speck, coarsely chopped
100 ml (3½ fl oz) olive oil
125 ml (½ cup) chicken stock
1 small handful oregano leaves
500 g (1 lb 2 oz) organic chicken liver, trimmed of all connective tissue
2½ tablespoons brandy
220 g (7¾ oz) unsalted Pepe Saya butter, diced
100 ml (3½ fl oz) Pepe Saya ghee
10 thyme sprigs

Sauté onion, garlic and speck in frying pan over medium–high heat with 2½ tablespoons olive oil for 5–10 minutes or until the onion is caramelised. Deglaze pan with chicken stock, scraping base of pan, and add oregano leaves. Transfer to a bowl.

Wipe pan clean, add remaining olive oil and place over high heat until hot. Add chicken liver and fry, turning halfway, for 4–6 minutes until browned and just firm, but pink on the inside. Add brandy, tilt pan to light it (if using a gas flame), or use a match, and flambé, stirring carefully for 1 minute or until the flames die out. Add onion mixture to the livers and stir for 1 minute. Season to taste with salt and freshly ground black pepper.

Remove from heat, cool slightly, then transfer to a blender or food processor. Blend, gradually adding the diced butter until smooth and combined. Pass through a fine sieve, pour into a terrine mould and chill for 15 minutes.

Heat ghee in a small saucepan over low heat until melted, then carefully pour it over the top of the pâté to seal the surface. Top with thyme — it will set into the ghee as it cools. Cover the terrine with plastic wrap and refrigerate overnight to set. Pâté will keep refrigerated for a week.

Jehan's summer salad with Wagyu chuck

'My parents migrated to Australia in the late 1960s from Lebanon. When I was growing up, fresh homemade food was always a focal point of weekend gatherings with extended family and friends. Also, my father has always had a garden with lots of fresh vegies and some fruit, so I think that's where my love of cooking comes from. This salad, combining vibrant, sweet vegies and tender barbecued meat, is typical of our summer dinners. The salad ingredients are pretty flexible, and you can always use a different protein, but we love this dish with juicy, pasture-fed and finished Wagyu chuck, a cut that is full of flavour. Just ensure your dressing is tangy and packed with lots of flavour to bring it all together.'

Jehan Abouhamad, retail customer

_____

Feeds: 4 | Preparation time: 20 minutes, plus cooling | Cooking time: 35 minutes

4 Wagyu chuck steaks (about 250 g/9 oz each), at room temperature
2 tablespoons coconut oil or olive oil

Salad

2 sweet potatoes, peeled, thinly sliced into rounds
2 tablespoons coconut oil or olive oil
2 tablespoons za'atar
2 lemons
1½ tablespoons maple syrup
100 g (3½ oz) mixed green leaves
1 cos lettuce, core removed, chopped
1 bunch flat-leaf parsley, finely chopped
250 g (9 oz) cherry tomatoes, halved
3 Lebanese (short) cucumbers, thinly sliced
5–6 radishes, trimmed and quartered
1 large fennel bulb (fronds reserved and coarsely chopped), thinly sliced
115 g (4 oz/¾ cup) pine nuts, toasted

Dressing

70 g (2½ oz/½ cup) walnuts
1 bunch flat-leaf parsley, coarsely chopped
1 bunch basil
1 small red chilli, finely chopped
½ garlic clove
1 cup (9 fl oz/250 ml) olive oil

Preheat oven to 160°C (315°F). To make the salad, line two large baking trays with baking paper. Toss sweet potatoes with oil and za'atar and spread them on one tray. Squeeze the lemons, reserving juice for the dressing, then coarsely chop the lemons. Toss them with maple syrup and spread them on the other tray. Roast for 25–30 minutes until sweet potato is golden and lemons are caramelised. Cool.

Meanwhile, to make the dressing, process walnuts in a small food processor until coarsely chopped. Transfer to a bowl, then process parsley, basil, chilli, garlic and reserved fennel fronds until finely chopped. Add oil, lemon juice and walnuts to herb mix and process until well combined. Season to taste with salt and pepper.

Preheat a barbecue grill to high. Brush steaks with oil, season with salt and grill for about 4 minutes each side for medium. Transfer to a plate, cover, and rest for 5 minutes.

Combine all the salad ingredients, except caramelised lemons and pine nuts, in a large bowl. Add some dressing, season to taste with salt and freshly ground black pepper, and toss very lightly to coat.

Cut the steaks across the grain into 1 cm (½ in) slices, season with salt and freshly ground black pepper, and add to the salad bowl. Drizzle with a little more dressing, toss everything together gently, and serve topped with caramelised lemons and pine nuts.

Michele's barbecued goat rump salad

'There is something about the neighbourhood "bring a plate" barbecue that brings together not only people and their stories, but also the cultural touchstones of traditional cuisines and family favourites. Where once it was pallid potatoes in mayonnaise and a strange rice salad that showed no allegiance to any country, we now find ourselves surrounded by spiced vegetables, tangy noodles, marinated meat, fried breads and a United Nations gathering of dips and nibbles. As a child growing up in a home of lamb chops and boiled vegetables, I still fondly recall the first time I went to a Greek neighbour's celebration that featured a spit-roasted lamb. It was noisy, a grapevine grew over the back door and I was handed a plate of parsley, oregano and succulent peppery meat drenched in lemon juice. That was it, I was on my first culinary adventure. The following recipe is a modern ode to that afternoon with spices, tangy citrus and zingy flavours.'

Michele Cranston, writer and chef

———

Feeds: 4 | Preparation time: 15 minutes, plus marinating | Cooking time: 1 hour

600 g (1 lb 5 oz) whole goat rump
2 tablespoons olive oil, plus extra
  for drizzling
1 tablespoon ras el hanout
½ Kent pumpkin (about 750 g/1 lb 10 oz),
  peeled and cut into wedges
1 red onion, cut into small wedges
100 g (3½ oz/½ cup) farro or spelt
2 celery stalks, thinly sliced
2 handfuls flat-leaf parsley leaves
2 handfuls coriander (cilantro) leaves
80 g (2¾ oz) ½ cup) pomegranate
  seeds (optional)

Dressing

3 tablespoons extra-virgin olive oil
1 tablespoon lemon juice
1 tablespoon finely chopped Indian lime
  pickle (from select supermarkets)
1 teaspoon nigella seeds

Combine dressing ingredients in a screw-top jar and shake well.

Trim goat of excess fat and make several deep incisions in the meat, to open the rump out. Rub olive oil and ras el hanout over the surface and season generously with freshly ground black pepper. Transfer to a bowl and refrigerate for several hours or overnight.

Preheat oven to 200°C (400°F). Preheat a barbecue grill to medium–high heat. Bring goat to room temperature.

Spread pumpkin and onion on a baking tray. Drizzle with extra oil, season with salt and freshly ground black pepper and roast for 30–35 minutes, until the edges start to burn a little. Leave to cool.

Meanwhile cook farro or spelt in a saucepan of boiling salted water for 25–30 minutes, until al dente. Drain and transfer to a bowl. Pour dressing over, add celery and herbs and toss to combine.

Grill goat on the barbecue, fat-side down, for 15 minutes, or until browned. Turn, cover with an upturned frying pan or metal bowl and cook for another 20 minutes for medium–rare, or until done to your liking. Season with salt, cover, and rest for 10 minutes.

Add roasted vegetables to the farro or spelt and transfer to a platter. Thinly slice the meat, arrange over the top and scatter with pomegranate seeds, if using.

Christopher's seared liver with tomatoes and caramelised onions

'I'm an artist, but my father was a butcher, and we had a nice little herd of Black Angus for a while. My first cooking job was to make the Saturday morning butcher's breakfast before I did the deliveries. So I used whatever morsels were around — liver, ends of bacon, kidneys, little lamb chops — fried them up in an old electric frying pan, then served them on a slab of thickly buttered bread. It was a tough gig, as butchers don't like their meat ruined, so timing was everything. I love good fresh liver, served medium–rare, with jammy onion and pan-roasted tomatoes. Sear the liver at the last minute while the sourdough bread is toasting.'

Christopher Hodges, retail customer

———

Feeds: 2–4 depending on the size of the liver | Preparation time: 15 minutes
Cooking time: 30 minutes

40 g (1½ oz) butter, plus extra
   for spreading
2 tablespoons olive oil
2–4 brown onions (1 per person), diced
250 g (9 oz/2 cups) cherry tomatoes,
   halved
1 lamb, goat or calf (veal) liver, rinsed,
   membrane removed, sliced into
   1.5 cm (⅝ in) strips
1 handful chopped flat-leaf
   parsley leaves
2–4 slices sourdough bread

Add a generous knob of butter to a frying pan over medium–high heat. Swirl for 2–3 minutes until lightly browned, then add a good dash of olive oil. Add onion and a large pinch of salt, reduce heat to medium–low, and cook, stirring gently, for 15–20 minutes. The onion will slowly turn golden, then brown, sweet and yummy.

Meanwhile, heat a separate frying pan over medium–high heat. Add tomatoes — they'll sizzle as they hit the pan — then add a bit more butter, season to taste with salt and freshly ground black pepper, and cook, turning once, for 5 minutes or until lightly browned and juicy.

Drizzle liver all over with remaining olive oil. Heat a heavy-based frying pan over medium–high heat, add liver and sear it quickly, without turning, for 1 minute until sealed and caramelised a little, then turn it quickly and sear for another minute until nicely browned but still rare in the middle. Transfer to a plate, season to taste with salt and freshly ground black pepper and top with parsley, then cover with an upturned bowl or a lid — it will keep cooking so by the time you serve it will be cooked through but still pink in the middle.

Meanwhile, toast sourdough in a toaster.

Butter toast, and top with onions, tomatoes and liver to serve.

Julian's Wiener schnitzel (like the Wieners do)

'Coming from a Viennese family the schnitzel has a place in my heart. This is my version, which comes from my stepmother's family as passed down to me from my father. The stereotypical Viennese schnitzel is made with milk-fed veal; however many Viennese households prefer a pork schnitzel. These traditional schnitzels are also cooked in lard, which is very typical in Viennese cooking and adds a heap of flavour.

Note that the lard takes time to melt and reach cooking temperature so don't leave it to the last minute — starting on low–medium heat in a heavy-based saucepan and then increasing the heat once melted, the lard will take half an hour or so to get up to the right temperature. Once the lard has cooled after cooking, strain it through a sieve into a jar and store in the fridge until the next time.

Serve with a potato salad and a fresh green salad. Prepare the potato salad an hour or more before cooking in order to allow the potatoes to absorb and mix with the dressing.'

Julian Schimmel, retail customer

———

Feeds: 4 | Preparation time: 25 minutes | Cooking time: 35 minutes

6–8 pork loin steaks, trimmed
  and cut into butterflied steaks about
  5 mm (¼ in) thick
3 eggs
150 g (5½ oz/1 cup) plain (all-purpose) flour
165 g (5¾ oz/1½ cups) fine dry
  breadcrumbs
500–750 g (1 lb 2 oz–1 lb 10 oz) lard
Lemon wedges and a green salad, to serve

Potato salad

700 g (1 lb 9 oz) kipfler potatoes
  (all roughly the same size)
2 small French shallots, finely chopped
3 tablespoons red wine vinegar
3 tablespoons olive oil
100 ml (3½ fl oz) chicken stock
  (preferably homemade), warmed
Chopped flat-leaf parsley leaves,
  to serve (optional)

To make the potato salad, steam potatoes over a saucepan of boiling water for 20–25 minutes until tender. Meanwhile, add shallot to vinegar and leave to macerate. When potatoes are done, remove from steamer and cool briefly on a plate. After a few minutes, put the plate in the fridge for 5–10 minutes to cool. When cool enough to handle, peel potatoes and cut into 5 mm–1 cm (¼–½ in) rounds. Add olive oil to vinegar and shallots, and add a generous sprinkle of salt and some freshly ground black pepper, then whisk together to emulsify.

Mix peeled (still slightly warm) potato rounds and dressing together with stock. Initially the mixture will be quite wet and soupy. After 5–10 minutes, mix it again gently with your hands to avoid the potatoes breaking up too much. After another 10 minutes, mix it again. After another mix or two the potatoes will absorb a lot of the liquid and the starch from the potatoes will also combine with the dressing to create a creamy texture. Shortly before serving, garnish with parsley.

For the schnitzels, place a piece of plastic wrap on a chopping board, top with a pork loin steak and cover with another piece of plastic wrap. Pound gently with a wooden meat mallet to flatten and tenderise the meat — don't use too much force; it shouldn't be pounded too thin, but should increase in size by about half. Repeat with remaining pork loin, season with salt, and set aside on a tray.

Crack eggs into a bowl and beat to combine, and place flour and breadcrumbs in separate bowls.

Melt enough lard over low–medium heat in a heavy-based saucepan to come 1 cm (½ in) up the side. Lard is ready when a pinch of breadcrumbs starts sizzling immediately when added. When lard is ready, increase heat to medium–high, take a piece of pork loin, dust it in flour, shaking off excess, then dip it in egg and coat it in breadcrumbs. Slide pork into the hot lard and immediately prepare another piece of pork and slide it into the lard. Depending on the size of your pan, you can cook two or three pieces at a time. Fry, turning every 30 seconds or so, for 3–4 minutes until deep golden brown; be careful, the lard will bubble vigorously. Remove schnitzels and let the lard drain before placing onto a warm plate lined with paper towel. Repeat with remaining pork.

Season schnitzels with a pinch of salt and serve with potato salad, lemon wedges and a green salad.

Shalini's South Indian goat fry

'My husband and I moved to Australia from Southern India two years ago. We tried lots of butchers but we couldn't find good goat meat until we came across Feather and Bone — it's the best thing we've found in Sydney. Our family and friends love it and we think the secret is the organic way it's grown and the fact that all the delicious fat is left on the meat. My husband is a strong believer of the traditional saying "health is wealth", and I agree with him. I don't want us to be running to the doctor for medicine so we cook all our own food with selected, mostly organic ingredients. We cook goat meat in several ways — we make goat curry, goat pepper fry, goat green chilli fry and goat dry roast. We prefer spicy food and this recipe is my husband's favourite. It's cooked slowly, step by step, and ends up being very juicy and tender, holding in all the aromatic flavours.'

Shalini Shiva, retail customer

———

Feeds: 4 | Preparation time: 10 minutes | Cooking time: 50 minutes

500 g (1 lb 2 oz) goat rump and/or leg (known as 'mutton' in parts of Asia), diced
1 teaspoon ground turmeric
½ cinnamon stick
4 cloves
1 cardamom pod
2 teaspoons ghee, plus extra as needed
3–4 curry leaf sprigs, leaves picked
4 long green chillies, chopped
1 brown onion, sliced
1 teaspoon ginger paste
1 teaspoon garlic paste
2 teaspoons ground chilli
1 teaspoon ground coriander (cilantro)
½ teaspoon garam masala
Coriander (cilantro) leaves, to serve
Steamed rice and lime wedges, to serve

Place the goat in a colander and rinse under cold water. Sprinkle with half the turmeric, toss to coat, and rinse it off with water.

Add goat to a large saucepan with cinnamon, cloves and cardamom, cover with water and bring to the boil, then reduce heat to medium and simmer for 30 minutes until cooked through. Drain, reserving cooking liquid.

Heat ghee in a large frying pan over medium heat. Add curry leaves and chilli. Cook, stirring, for 2–3 minutes until softened, then add onion and fry, stirring occasionally, for 5 minutes or until transparent. Add ginger and garlic, and cook, stirring for 2 minutes, then add ground chilli, coriander, garam masala, remaining turmeric and 2 teaspoons salt and stir to combine.

Increase heat to medium–high, add goat and fry, stirring occasionally and adding more ghee if necessary, for 5 minutes or until browned. Add 3 tablespoons reserved cooking liquid and simmer, stirring occasionally, for 5 minutes or until the stock is evaporated. Stir in coriander leaves and serve with rice and lime wedges.

Wendy's Norwegian lamb shanks

'Animal welfare from birth to death is a high priority for me, as is sustainable farming, and so Feather and Bone is a godsend, with the assurance of Grant's regular tours of inspection. The Norwegian lamb shanks are a much-anticipated favourite from childhood, as cooked by my mother, Joan Copeland. And if Feather and Bone is out of lamb shanks (remember how few legs each sheep actually has!), any part of the lamb will do. These are always extra special with a fresh bay leaf from the bay tree given to me by my middle child, Hannah.

(When I was a time-strapped mum with hungry children, I used to omit the stages of putting the dish in the fridge and making the roux; instead I simply added the sour cream and dill, and then served with rice and whatever vegetables were on hand.)'

Wendy Bowring, retail customer

———

Feeds: 6 | Preparation time: 10 minutes | Cooking time: 2 hours, plus chilling

6 lamb shanks, trimmed
90 g (3¼ oz) butter (or 60 g/2¼ oz
  if you wish to omit the roux)
1 large brown onion, chopped
375 ml (13 fl oz/1½ cups) dry white wine
375 ml (13 fl oz/1½ cups) lamb or
  beef stock
1 bay leaf
30 g (1 oz) plain (all-purpose) flour
  (if you make the roux)
3 tablespoons chopped dill
245 g (9 oz/1 cup) sour cream
Boiled new potatoes and a cucumber
  salad, to serve

Season lamb shanks with salt and freshly ground black pepper. Heat 60 g butter in a large frying pan over medium–high heat, add shanks, in batches if necessary, and fry, turning occasionally, for 10 minutes or until browned all over. Transfer to a casserole dish, leaving the drippings in the frying pan.

Add onion to the frying pan with dripping, reduce heat to medium and cook gently, stirring occasionally, for about 5 minutes or until soft and translucent. Pour in wine and 125 ml of the stock and bring to the boil. Transfer to casserole dish with bay leaf.

Cover and simmer over medium–low heat for 1½ hours or until shanks are tender. Cool to room temperature, then transfer to the refrigerator to chill. Remove any fat that sets on top.

Reheat casserole over medium heat, remove shanks, and keep warm in a low oven. Add remaining butter to casserole, stir until melted, then add flour and stir for 2 minutes until sandy coloured. Gradually stir in the rest of the stock, and simmer for 3–5 minutes until mixture boils and thickens.

Stir in dill and sour cream, season to taste with salt and freshly ground black pepper, return lamb shanks to casserole and turn to coat. Serve with potatoes and cucumber salad.

Wendy's roast pork belly with crackling

Feeds: 8–10 | Preparation time: 10 minutes | Cooking time: 1½ hours

Olive oil, for drizzling
2 brown onions, cut into 1 cm (½ in) slices
2 sweet potatoes, halved lengthways then
   cut into 1 cm (½ in) slices
2 apples, halved
1.5 kg (3 lb 8 oz) boneless pork belly
250 ml (9 fl oz/1 cup) apple cider
Steamed green vegetables, to serve

Preheat oven to 190°C (375°F). Drizzle a little oil in a ceramic baking dish. Spread onions on the base, add a layer of sweet potato, and top with apple, skin-side up.

Pat pork belly dry with paper towel. Score the skin at 1–1.5 cm (½ in) intervals without cutting into the flesh. Rub skin with a little olive oil and sea salt. Place pork on top of the other ingredients.

Roast for 45 minutes, then add cider, pouring it beside the pork rather than on top of it, and roast for another 45 minutes until the pork belly is tender and cooked through, with a delicious, crunchy crackling. Rest for 10 minutes, then serve with steamed greens.

Charlotte's lazy roast chook

'I'm an enthusiastic but lazy cook — and there's no better dish for such a person than roast chicken, the most versatile meat dish I can think of. You can splash the panache with fancy ingredients, posh salads and micro-herbs, or channel your inner nanna and go old-school with a stodgy gravy and roast spuds. It can feed three people or 10, the leftovers will never be wasted, and you can make stock from the bones. This method involves a teeny bit of effort for a lot of joy.'

Charlotte Wood, retail customer

———

Feeds: 4–6 | Preparation time: 15 minutes, plus drying | Cooking time: 1½ hours

1 whole chicken (about 1.8 kg/4 lb)
50 g (1¾ oz) unsalted butter, softened
5 garlic cloves, 2 cloves finely chopped
1 handful of finely chopped herbs (thyme, rosemary, parsley — whatever you have on hand)
Olive oil, for drizzling
2 lemons, cut in half
2 fennel bulbs, thickly sliced
2 leeks, white parts only, thickly sliced
1 tablespoon white wine

Pat chicken dry with paper towel and leave uncovered in the fridge for 30 minutes to 1 hour to dry out the skin.

Preheat oven to 200°C (400°F). Add butter, chopped garlic and herbs to a bowl, season with sea salt, and mix until well combined. With your fingers, gently separate the skin of the chicken breast from the flesh and work most of the butter underneath, being careful not to break the skin. Massage it gently to spread it evenly. Smooth any extra butter over the outside of the chicken with a little olive oil, squeeze the juice of 1 lemon over and season with salt. Place garlic, remaining lemon, and any more herbs you have around into the cavity.

Toss fennel and leek in olive oil and spread in a roasting tin. Sit the chicken on top, place in oven with legs facing to the back and roast for 45 minutes to 1 hour until the juices run clear when a thigh is pierced with a skewer. Transfer chicken to a warm dish, turn it breast-side down, cover loosely with foil and rest for 20 minutes. While the bird is resting, throw a bit of white wine into the pan with the vegetables and stir to deglaze. Carve chicken into large pieces.

Spread roasted fennel and leek on a platter, place chicken on top and pour over any pan juices. Serve with whatever other veg you like, but if you really want to be loved make sure to include some crisp roasted potatoes.

When dinner is over, you can keep the carcass and any remaining bones and throw them into a pot of water with some vegetables and herbs to make a stock.

Valentyna's oyster blade with green sauce

'If you'd said to teenage me that I would grow up to be a farmer, I probably would have laughed, but here I am. Sydney's inner west seems aeons away from our farm in the Upper Hunter Valley of New South Wales, where my partner and I farm Black Galloways. As farmers, we are committed to leaving our patch of paradise in better health than when we found it.

One of the ironies of our life as beef farmers is that well hung, carefully butchered animals are often difficult to access. When we do have some available, we opt for cuts such as flank, shin and chuck, enjoying their deeper flavour. Oyster blade is delicious slow-roasted to break down its middle membrane and connective tissue, but prepared and hung properly, it responds beautifully to a quick cook. At home we would cook this on a fire and serve it with whatever the garden and hills have to offer at the time. On the stovetop, a cast-iron pan lightly brushed with oil and heated until wisps of smoke rise can give pretty good results, too.'

Valentyna Juskin, farmer and retail customer

———

Feeds: 4 | Preparation time: 10 minutes | Cooking time: 15 minutes
Special equipment: A grill plate, or two large cast-iron frying pans

4 oyster blade steaks (about 250–300 g/
  9–10 oz each), at room temperature
Boiled new potatoes and steamed green
  beans, to serve

Green sauce

Handful finely chopped mixed soft herbs,
  such as flat-leaf parsley, dill, tarragon,
  mint and chives
110 g (3¾ oz/½ cup) pitted and finely
  chopped green olives
Finely grated zest and juice of 2 lemons
2 garlic cloves, crushed
250 ml (9 fl oz/1 cup) olive oil
Dijon mustard, to taste

To make the green sauce, take the time to finely chop herbs and olives by hand, to ensure your sauce doesn't taste like the smell of lawn clippings. Combine in a bowl with lemon zest, lemon juice and garlic. Add enough olive oil to make a loose dressing, then add mustard, salt and freshly ground black pepper to taste.

If you're cooking the steak over a fire, make sure your coals are white-hot and the grill plate is smoking. If using the stovetop, you may need to use two cast-iron pans; make sure they are super-hot and well seasoned, so the steaks don't stick.

Season steaks on both sides with salt and place on the grill or in your pan/s. Cook for about 6 minutes, turn, then cook for a further 6 minutes until browned. Depending on their thickness, this should get you to medium–rare, which is perfect.

When the steaks are cooked to your liking, remove from the grill, let them rest for 5 minutes, then slice across the grain and season to taste with salt.

Serve with the green sauce and potatoes and beans.

John's marinated, butterflied lamb leg Podere Caporlese style

'I came across a meat marinade including fish sauce when I was staying with a friend in Umbria (Podere Caporlese is the name of her farmhouse) in 1988. She was a wonderful cook with a fantastic vegetable garden so we ate lots of simple vegetable pasta sauces and not much meat — sometimes pork and occasionally lamb, which wasn't freely available. When we could buy lamb, my friend made a marinade of garlic, rosemary, fish sauce and olive oil, and left the meat to marinate for a day.'

John May, retail customer

———

Feeds: 6 | Preparation time: 10 minutes, plus marinating
Cooking time: 20–30 minutes

6 garlic cloves
2 handfuls rosemary leaves
2½ tablespoons fish sauce
150 ml (5 fl oz) olive oil
Moorlands biodynamic Texel butterflied
   lamb leg (about 1.8–2 kg/4 lb–4 lb 6 oz)
Smashed roasted potatoes and a crisp
   green salad, to serve

Blend garlic, rosemary, fish sauce and olive oil with a stick blender or in a small food processor to a creamy consistency.

Place lamb in a large non-reactive bowl and spread marinade all over. Cover and refrigerate overnight to marinate.

Preheat oven to 200°C (400°F) and bring lamb to room temperature. Place lamb on a wire rack in a roasting tin and roast for 30 minutes or until browned and cooked to your liking. (Alternatively, cook lamb on a barbecue over high heat for 20–30 minutes.) Rest for 10 minutes, then serve with smashed roasted potatoes and a crisp green salad.

Jane's crisp roast pork hock with spiced red cabbage and apple horseradish

'Cooking this dish whisks me back to Munich where I tasted my first brutish Schweinshaxe in the nineties. Immediately I realised the need to recreate it in Australia where the cut, translating as pork knuckles or shanks, is under-utilised. My partially Germanic blood craves spiced red cabbage as a natural partner and the addition of apples and horseradish beautifully balances the pork's richness. Low, slow simmering tenderises the well-worked lower leg muscle and chilling until dry before frying results in premium crackle.'

Jane Lawson, writer and chef

———

Feeds: 4 | Preparation time: 20 minutes | Cooking time: 1½ hours

4 x 750 g (1 lb 10 oz) fresh pork hocks from the hind legs, lightly scored around the hock
2 tablespoons sea salt

Spiced red cabbage

60 g (2¼ oz) butter
1 red onion, thinly sliced
1.5 kg (3 lb 5 oz/about ½ large head) red cabbage, core removed, coarsely shredded
65 g (2½ oz/½ cup) dried cranberries
1 Granny Smith apple, peeled, cored and grated
6 juniper berries
3 tablespoons red wine
3 tablespoons red wine vinegar
1 bay leaf
½ teaspoon freshly grated nutmeg
3 tablespoons brown sugar
½ teaspoon ground allspice

Apple horseradish

3 tablespoons apple sauce
2 tablespoons bottled horseradish

Preheat oven to 220°C (425°F). Place a large wire rack in a roasting tin. Stand hocks upright on the rack, balancing them against each other with the small end pointing up. Rub well with sea salt. Cook for 1 hour, then reduce temperature to 160°C (315°F). Pour a small amount of water into the tin under the rack and cook for 1 hour further. Increase the temperature to 220°C (425°F) and cook for a further 30 minutes, or until pork is very tender, dark golden and crisp. Remove from the oven, cover, and rest for about 10 minutes before serving.

While the hocks are cooking, make the spiced red cabbage. Melt butter in a large saucepan over medium–high heat. Add onion and cabbage and stir for 10 minutes, or until cabbage has wilted slightly. Add the rest of the ingredients, except allspice, and stir to combine. Cover with a lid, reduce the heat to low and simmer for 40 minutes, stirring occasionally, until cabbage is tender and there is very little liquid left. Stir in allspice and season with salt and freshly ground black pepper to taste. Turn off the heat and cover to keep warm.

Combine apple sauce and horseradish and mix well.

Serve hocks on top of some cabbage with the apple horseradish sauce on the side.

Matt and Ceinwen's picanha with pear, pecan and radicchio salad

'We were vegetarians until a few years ago. Ceinwen hadn't eaten meat for decades and in 2008 I was shocked into vegetarianism by the documentary *Food Inc*, which exposed the unethical and exploitative practices of industrial-scale crop and livestock production. By contrast, I'd spent time on my grandfather's farm as a kid so I knew what good small-scale farming looked like.

It wasn't the reality of eating animals that bothered me so much as the systems in which most meat is produced. But in 2015, when Ceinwen was pregnant with Jack, she realised she needed more iron, which meant more meat — a big decision for us. So we found ourselves at Feather and Bone and now our family of four (Jack has a sister, Bonnie) eat a small amount of locally sourced, pasture-raised meat each week. Buying from a whole-body butchery gives you the opportunity to explore different cuts, which is how we ended up trying picanha, or rump cap. If the ingredients are good, you don't need to do much with them — just get out of their way and let them shine.'

Matt Harrington and Ceinwen Berry, retail customers

———

Feeds: 4 | Preparation time: 10 minutes | Cooking time: 45 minutes
Special equipment: A charcoal barbecue

1 kg (2 lb 4 oz) piece picanha (rump cap), at room temperature
1 tablespoon olive oil
20 g (¾ oz) butter
2 teaspoons maple syrup
100 g (3½ oz/1 cup) pecans
1 head radicchio
Juice of ½ lemon
2 tablespoons extra-virgin olive oil
1 firm pear
Shaved parmesan, to serve
Aged balsamic vinegar, to serve

Score the fat side of the picanha at 2 cm (¾ in) intervals to form a cross-hatch pattern. Rub a generous amount of salt flakes onto the fat side and rub the flesh side with olive oil. Season all over with salt and freshly ground black pepper to taste.

If you have a charcoal barbecue, set it up for indirect grilling, with a hot zone and another with more gentle, indirect heat. If you're using a gas barbecue, preheat the grill to high.

Recipe continued over page
→

*Matt and Ceinwen's
picanha with pear, pecan
and radicchio salad.*

Once the coals reach high heat (you should only be able to hold your hand above the coals for a second or two), sear the picanha over direct heat, fat-side first and turning halfway, for 5–10 minutes until browned. Move the picanha to an indirect position (or turn the heat to low on a gas barbecue and close the lid) and cook for 25–35 minutes for medium–rare, or until cooked to your liking. Transfer to a plate and rest for 10–15 minutes.

Meanwhile, to make the salad, melt butter with maple syrup in a frying pan over low heat. Add pecans and toss for 3–5 minutes until roasted and the butter reduces and turns sticky. Be careful, it can burn quickly. Tumble the pecans onto paper towel and let them cool.

Tear radicchio into a shallow serving bowl, add lemon juice and extra-virgin olive oil and toss to coat, seasoning to taste with salt flakes. Halve and core the pear, then thinly slice it. Spread pear over leaves, top with pecans and shaved parmesan and drizzle with balsamic vinegar to taste.

Carve the picanha across the grain in 2 cm (¾ in) slices and pour the juice over the sliced meat. Serve with the salad and a cleansing ale.

Jessica and Antony's sausage and cavolo nero ragu

'Having worked for many years in hospitality, it is important to us that our meat is sourced ethically, from producers who are passionate about caring for their animals and the land, even though we only eat meat once or twice a week. This comforting dish is especially tasty on a cold, wet night paired with a bottle of Chianti. It works so well because the flavour is driven by the seasoning and the quality of the Feather and Bone pastured pork used in the sausages.'

Jessica and Antony George, retail customers

———

Feeds: 4 | Preparation time: 10 minutes, plus soaking | Cooking time: 40 minutes

6 good-quality pastured pork sausages
90 ml (3 fl oz) extra-virgin olive oil, plus extra to serve
¼ teaspoon dried chilli flakes
1 small brown onion, finely chopped
2 garlic cloves, finely chopped
20 g (¾ oz) dried porcini mushrooms, rehydrated in warm water for 15 minutes, then drained and finely chopped
400 g (14 oz) tinned plum tomatoes
500 g (1 lb 2 oz) dried rigatoni or casarecce
1 bunch cavolo nero, finely shredded, blanched in boiling salted water for 1–2 minutes until tender, then drained well
60 g (2¼ oz) Parmigiano Reggiano, finely grated

Squeeze sausage meat from casings into a large, cold frying pan. Break into small lumps with a wooden spoon, add olive oil and place pan over medium heat. Gently fry, stirring regularly to break up the meat, for 5 minutes or until it starts to brown. Add chilli flakes and onion. Cook, stirring, for 4–5 minutes until onion is soft but not browned; reduce heat if necessary. Add garlic and porcini and cook, stirring, for 1–2 minutes until the mixture is fragrant, glossy and combined.

Reduce heat to low. Add tomatoes, stirring and breaking them up until completely dissolved into the sauce (or leave some in pieces if you prefer a chunkier style). Cover and gently simmer, stirring regularly, for about 20 minutes until thickened and reduced. You want a nice loose texture, so if it gets too thick add a little water.

Meanwhile, cook pasta in a large saucepan of boiling salted water according to packet instructions. About 7–8 minutes before the pasta is ready, stir cavolo nero through the ragu, along with 2–3 tablespoons pasta cooking water to loosen. Season to taste with salt and pepper and continue to simmer gently with the lid on.

Just before the pasta is done, take the ragu off the heat and stir in half the parmesan, with a little more pasta water if needed to keep the sauce nice and loose. Drain pasta, reserving some of the water. Stir pasta through the ragu, loosen with a final splash of pasta water and serve in warm bowls, topped with remaining parmesan and a drizzle of olive oil.

Norman's chicken heart Bolognese

'I'm a feeder. I love to cook for family and friends, an obsession passed onto me from my grandma or *por por*. I grew up in Hong Kong and spent much of my childhood in the kitchen with *por por*, preparing for the relatives to come and feast. I first discovered Feather and Bone in 2006, and I knew I'd found a kindred spirit when Grant started talking animatedly about pigs' heads. I told him about my grandmother's pig's head terrine; he told me about curing pork jowls and lardo. Over time I've established an enduring friendship with Grant and Laura, and somewhere along the way I learned to place value in how the animals we eat are treated, how farming can be regenerative, the importance of the whole animal and the potential of supporting a different food system.

Eating offal can often be associated with frugality but these days I find myself actively seeking it because of its supreme flavour. I make my Bolognese with chicken heart not just because it's cheaper than mince, but because I find this Bolognese to be more meaty, more savoury, and ultimately more tasty. Try it and see.'

Norman Lee, retail customer

———

Feeds: 4–6 | Preparation time: 20 minutes | Cooking time: 3 hours

1 tablespoon olive oil
2 brown onions, finely diced
1 carrot, finely diced
1 celery stalk, finely diced
100 g (3½ oz) pancetta (or bacon), finely diced
2 bay leaves
1 star anise
750 ml (26 fl oz/3 cups) tomato passata
1 kg (2 lb 4 oz) chicken hearts, untrimmed, minced
250 g (9 oz) chicken liver (optional), minced
2 tablespoons milk
Pasta or crusty bread, to serve

Preheat oven to 140°C (275°F). Take a heavy-based ovenproof saucepan and cut out a round of baking paper to fit in the pan. Set paper aside. Heat olive oil in the pan over medium heat. Add onions, carrot, celery and a large pinch of salt. Cook, stirring, for 5–10 minutes until softened and lightly caramelised. Add pancetta and cook, stirring occasionally, for 3–5 minutes until fat has rendered. Add bay leaves and star anise and stir to combine, then pour in passata and bring to a simmer. Add mince, breaking it up roughly with a wooden spoon, and bring the mixture back to a gentle simmer.

Cover the sauce with the circle of baking paper and transfer to the middle shelf of the oven. Bake for 2–3 hours until the sauce is reduced and thickened. Season to taste with salt and freshly ground black pepper. Stir in any crusty bits that have formed on the edge and add a dash of milk just before serving.

Serve over pasta or with crusty bread of your choice.

Laura's grandma's Cornish pasties, page 213.

8.

You could do this

Longer and slower
but not harder

*Everything from rich hearty stews
and smoky ribs to pig's ear banh mi
and nurturing bone broth.*

Matthew's ribs with Sadie's barbecue sauce

'Sadie's family, on her dad's side, comes from Oklahoma, and this is a simpler variation of their barbecue sauce, which we first published in Fat Pig Farm's book of preserves, *Not Just Jam*. It's a tomato-based sauce, but the secret is the pureed lemon, which adds piquancy to the spices. You want your ribs slow cooked, so they are tender enough to chew easily, but not wet so the bones all fall out. It's home cooking at its best.'

Matthew Evans and Sadie Chrestman, producers and chefs

———

Feeds: 6–8 | Preparation time: 10 minutes | Cooking time: 2½ hours

1 tablespoon olive oil
½ small brown or red onion, finely diced
1 teaspoon finely grated ginger
½ teaspoon cumin seeds
1 teaspoon ground coriander (cilantro)
1 tablespoon hot paprika
   (or use sweet and some chilli)
½ lemon, finely chopped,
   plus juice of 1 lemon
2 tablespoons brown sugar
1 teaspoon mustard powder
400 g (14 oz) tinned crushed
   Italian tomatoes
1 tablespoon Worcestershire sauce
6 whole 9-rib racks of pork ribs

Heat olive oil in a large, heavy-based saucepan over low heat. Add onion and fry, stirring occasionally, for 5 minutes or until soft. Add ginger, cumin, coriander and paprika and fry gently for 5 minutes or until fragrant, stirring occasionally. Don't let the spices brown and burn. Add all remaining ingredients, except ribs, with 1 teaspoon salt and simmer gently, stirring occasionally and adding a little water if the pan is drying out, for 15 minutes or until flavours have combined.

Rub ribs all over with the marinade. It'd be good to do this a day ahead; if so, cover and refrigerate until ready to cook.

Preheat oven to 150°C (300°F). Place ribs, curved-side down, in two roasting tins with 3 cm (1¼ in) sides, trying to separate the racks as much as possible so they're not a tall stack. Add 125 ml (4 fl oz/½ cup) water, cover ribs with baking paper, then tightly with foil. Bake for 1 hour, changing the stacking every 20 minutes so the top rack goes to the bottom and the rest move up.

Turn ribs over, re-cover and bake for another 20 minutes, then remove paper and foil. Continue to bake, basting every 5–10 minutes, for about 30–40 minutes, until ribs are browned and pulling apart easily — add a touch more water to the pan if it starts to stick, and again move the ribs around so they all get some time on the top of the pile to get colour. It's a balancing act between browning the ribs and not drying them out. Be sure the marinade is on the ribs, not the pan, and is baked on nicely.

Serve with paper napkins because you're going to get a big greasy grin eating them.

Feather and Bone's put-your-feet-up meat sauce

If you're like us, the quest to achieve a sane work/life balance sometimes feels like a cross between an extreme sport practised by certified lunatics and a form of medieval torture. So it's critical to have something nutritious in the freezer that you can whip out to tame the hordes on those nights when everyone's at breaking point. This is our answer — a crowd-pleasing, healthy sauce made with a hearty, nutritious beef broth. Make it on Sunday afternoon, let it simmer away gently while you do something nice, then tuck it away in the freezer in serves. Serve it with pasta or rice, add it to a ratatouille, pile it into tacos, spoon it into iceberg lettuce leaves, bake it topped with mashed potato and parsnip and grated parmesan, or go full teenager and dollop it into a roll. The options are endless. Add more herbs or vegetables or an extra nutritional punch by including some offal in the mince — it adds a wonderful depth to the flavour and they'll never know they're eating offal. (Or go the whole way with Norman's chicken heart Bolognese, page 177.) Good broth and long, slow cooking is the secret here.

Makes: 3.5 kg/about 7 x 500 g containers that each feed 3–4 people
(depending on whether or not your house includes multiple teenage boys)
Preparation time: 15 minutes | Cooking time: 3 hours

200 ml (7 fl oz) extra-virgin olive oil
2 small carrots (about 200 g/7 oz),
 finely diced
3–4 celery stalks (about 200 g/7 oz),
 finely diced
2 brown onions (about 300 g/10½ oz),
 finely diced
8–10 garlic cloves (about 40 g/1½ oz),
 crushed
200 g (7 oz) speck, rind removed, diced
1 kg (1 lb 2 oz) minced beef
125 ml (4 fl oz/½ cup) red wine
160 ml (5¼ fl oz) white wine
800 ml (28 fl oz) beef stock
1.2 kg (2 lb 10 oz) tomato passata
 or tinned crushed tomatoes
100 g (3½ oz) tomato paste
3 teaspoons dried oregano
4 fresh bay leaves

Heat olive oil in a large saucepan over medium heat, add carrot, celery, onion, garlic and speck, and sweat, stirring occasionally, for 5–10 minutes until vegetables have softened but not browned; the time this takes will depend on how finely your vegetables are diced.

Increase heat to high and add mince, stirring and breaking it up as it fries, until browned and starting to catch on the bottom — about 5 minutes or so. Add red and white wine and stock, then tomato passata and tomato paste. Stir well, then add oregano, bay leaves and 2 teaspoons salt.

Let the sauce come up to the boil, then reduce to a low simmer, put the lid on and simmer for about 3 hours until thick, rich and reduced. Eat it within a couple of days or freeze for up to 3 months.

Phillip's pot roast of beef

'I'm an Anglo Australian and one side of the family has been in NSW since 1800 with some of them still farming on the original 1822 land grant near Bathurst. I grew up in Sydney in the 1960s and 1970s and during my childhood, my mother bought 'rolled beef' at the corner butcher for a pot roast. The liquid was water and my mother never used garlic or chilli in anything, and none of us had even heard of ancho chilli. This recipe takes my mother's traditional pot roast and gives it a contemporary Australian spin. It's a guaranteed favourite at our house, but you can't rush it — slow-cooking what can be a tougher cut of beef yields a succulent result that's definitely worth the wait.

You can cook this recipe in the oven or on the stove — I find the oven easier. In our house, we don't add salt to anything so this recipe doesn't include salt. If you like to add salt while cooking, then do so to suit your taste.'

Phillip Sheard, retail customer

Feeds: 8 | Preparation time: 15 minutes | Cooking time: 4 hours
Special equipment: Kitchen string

3 tablespoons extra-virgin olive oil
1.5 kg (3 lb 5 oz) piece boneless chuck, tied with kitchen string (you may need to order ahead from your butcher)
2 brown onions, thinly sliced
300 ml (10½ fl oz) red wine or verjuice
150 ml (5 fl oz) beef stock
2 garlic cloves
1–2 long red chillies (optional)
2 small dried ancho chillies or dried red chillies
2 teaspoons black peppercorns
2 bay leaves

Preheat oven to 160°C (315°F). Heat olive oil in a large, heavy-based saucepan over high heat, add chuck and sear, turning, for 8–10 minutes or until browned all over. Remove beef from pan and set aside on a plate.

Reduce heat to medium, add onion and cook, stirring regularly, for 10 minutes or until soft and golden. Return beef to pan, add wine and enough stock or water to come two-thirds of the way up the side of the beef. Add garlic, chillies, peppercorns and bay leaves, increase heat to high and bring to a simmer.

Cover with a lid, transfer to oven and roast, turning the pan every 30–40 minutes, for 3½ hours, until beef is very tender. Remove beef from saucepan and transfer to a plate for 10 minutes to rest.

While beef is resting, place saucepan with cooking juices over high heat, bring to the boil and cook, scraping the base with a wooden spoon, for 5–10 minutes or until reduced to your liking. A thicker sauce will have a more intense flavour. Remove the dried chillies.

Carve the meat, removing the kitchen string, and spoon over some of the reduced sauce. Serve with remaining reduced sauce on the side.

Richie's beef brisket with egg noodles and greens

'When I was learning how to cook Chinese food, this was my go-to recipe, so different from the European or American methods, but so delicious. This is a great winter dish but you can lighten it with lime so it's good in warmer weather too.'

Richie Hughes, retail customer

———

Feeds: 6–8 | Preparation time: 15 minutes | Cooking time: 2½ hours
Special equipment: A large heavy-based saucepan, muslin (cheesecloth), kitchen string

2 tablespoons sunflower oil
1.5 kg (3 lb 5 oz) piece beef brisket, fat trimmed, cut into 5 cm (2 in) cubes
3 garlic cloves, finely chopped
2 cm (¾ in) piece ginger, thinly sliced
2 small French shallots, finely chopped
2–3 tablespoons chu hou sauce (available from select supermarkets and Asian grocers)
1 tablespoon dark soy sauce
400 ml (14 fl oz) beef or chicken stock
2 tablespoons rock sugar
1 daikon, cut into 2 cm (¾ in) cubes
Cooked egg noodles, stir-fried greens, oyster sauce and sesame oil, to serve
Coriander (cilantro) leaves, sansho powder (optional, from select Asian grocers) and lime wedges, to serve

Spice mix

3 star anise
2 bay leaves
1 teaspoon Sichuan peppercorns
1 teaspoon black peppercorns
1 small chipotle chilli
½ teaspoon fennel seeds

For the spice mix, wrap all ingredients in a piece of muslin (cheesecloth) and tie with kitchen string.

Heat half the oil in a large, heavy-based saucepan over high heat. Add beef in batches and fry, turning, for 8–10 minutes until well browned. Remove from pan. Add remaining oil to pan, reduce heat to medium, add garlic, ginger and shallots and fry, stirring, for 2–3 minutes until softened.

Return beef to pan and add chu hou sauce, soy sauce, stock and sugar. Stir to combine, add spice bag and simmer over medium–low heat for 1 hour. Taste braise and adjust sugar and salt to taste, then simmer, adding a little water if necessary, for a further 30 minutes or until meat is tender, but still has some texture. Add daikon and simmer for 30 minutes until tender.

Dress the egg noodles and greens with a little oyster sauce and sesame oil and divide among bowls. Spoon braise over, top with coriander and sansho powder and serve with lime wedges.

Ingrid's smoky, sweet and sour lamb ribs

'My family are Chinese-Indonesian and Mum's Chinese and Indonesian dishes were always delicious but the cooking looked complicated, so I left it to her. When I moved away for university, my love of food (i.e. eating) forced me to ditch the packet pasta and toasties, and led me to research recipes to create the delicious food I grew up with.

Today, I look for sustainably-raised produce, which allows for quicker and simpler cooking methods with the flavours coming direct from the produce itself! This recipe comes from a usual Saturday morning visit to Feather and Bone and seeing a beautiful set of lamb ribs, speaking to the butcher, discussing the cut, cooking methods and collaborating on how to create a sweet, spicy and smoky dish.'

Ingrid Oey, retail customer

_____

Feeds: 4 | Preparation time: 15 minutes, plus marinating
Cooking time: 2 hours 15 minutes

2 x 750 g (1 lb 10 oz) racks lamb ribs

Spice rub

2 tablespoons ground cumin
1 tablespoon smoked paprika
2 garlic cloves, crushed
1 teaspoon onion powder
1 sprig rosemary leaves, picked
½ teaspoon cayenne pepper (optional)
½ teaspoon salt
A good grind of black pepper
Peeled rind of 1 lemon
2 tablespoons coconut sugar
  (or brown sugar)
80 ml (2½ fl oz/⅓ cup) olive oil
2 drops liquid smoke (only if you have it,
  and only if you like it extra smoky)

Basting sauce

1 tablespoon honey
Juice of 1 lemon
Dash of apple cider vinegar

To make the spice rub, combine all ingredients in a bowl.

Place ribs in a shallow roasting tin and massage spice rub into lamb. Refrigerate, covered, for at least 1 hour to marinate.

When ready to cook, bring ribs to room temperature and preheat oven to 140°C (275°F). Cover roasting tin tightly with foil and bake for 2 hours or until tender and falling off the bone. Remove ribs from oven, and increase heat to 180°C (350°F).

When ribs are cool enough to handle, cut them into individual ribs. Stir basting sauce ingredients together in a bowl, then brush all over ribs. Place a wire rack in the roasting tin, spread ribs over the rack (it's fine if some overlap), then roast for 15 minutes until glazed and sticky.

Geezer's pork vindaloo

'Growing up in England, we had access to some of the best Indian food so my vindaloo education started early and became an abiding passion. As young punks, we'd go to our favourite Indian restaurant several times a week and later, when I trained as a chef, I learned how to make it myself. This is my personal interpretation, honed over many years. Vindaloo was invented by the Portuguese in Goa and is notorious for being hot and spicy.'

Ian 'Geezer' Sharp, retail customer

———

Feeds: 4 | Preparation time: 20 minutes, plus marinating | Cooking time: 2 hours

1.5 kg (3 lb 5 oz) pork shoulder,
   cut into 2.5 cm (1 in) dice, bone
   reserved (ask your butcher)
3 tablespoons vegetable oil
2 brown onions, finely sliced
10 garlic cloves, finely sliced
5 cm (2 in) piece ginger,
   cut into matchsticks
4 green chillies, chopped
400 g (14 oz) tinned chopped tomatoes
2 tablespoons black (Chinkiang) vinegar
   or malt vinegar
1 teaspoon jaggery or soft brown sugar
Mint, coriander (cilantro), lime wedges
   and steamed rice, to serve

Spice paste

2 tablespoons vegetable oil
6 cardamom pods, crushed, husks removed
1 teaspoon black peppercorns
4 dried red chillies
1 teaspoon cloves
1 cinnamon stick, roughly broken
2 teaspoons cumin
½ teaspoon coriander seeds
½ teaspoon fenugreek seeds
1 star anise, broken
2 tablespoons white vinegar

To make the spice paste, heat oil in a frying pan over medium heat. Add spices and fry, stirring, for 3–5 minutes until swollen and fragrant. Cool, then finely grind in a spice grinder or with a mortar and pestle. In a large bowl, combine ground spices with white vinegar.

Add pork to spice paste and toss to coat well. Cover and refrigerate for 3 hours to marinate.

Heat oil in a large, heavy-based saucepan over low heat, add onion and fry, stirring, for 5 minutes until lightly browned. Add garlic, ginger and chilli, and stir well.

Add pork, increase heat to high, and fry, turning, for 3–5 minutes or until browned. Add tomatoes, Chinkiang or malt vinegar, 250 ml (9 fl oz/1 cup) water and any of the marinade liquid left in the bowl. Reduce the heat to medium and slowly bring back to the boil.

Add jaggery and pork bone. Cover tightly and simmer, stirring occasionally, for about 1½ hours or until the meat is very tender.

Discard bone. Season with salt to taste and serve with herbs, lime, rice and your favourite vegetable dish.

Romany's Sri Lankan black beef curry

'I am a Sri Lankan-born chef and I am actually a vegetarian, but I have always been fascinated by butchery. The structure of the bones and muscles, the way the animal is put together, is a beautiful thing to see. I cook a lot of meat dishes for friends and family, and they always tell me what works best. This curry is thick and dark with a sour, spicy flavour and it provides a great counterpoint to the many sweet and creamy curries of Sri Lanka.'

Romany de Silva, chef

Feeds: 6 | Preparation time: 15 minutes, plus marinating | Cooking time: 2 hours

1 kg (2 lb 4 oz) diced beef blade or chuck
50 g (1¾ oz/½ cup) dark Sri Lankan curry powder (available from Sri Lankan grocers — make sure to get the dark powder)
3 teaspoons ground chilli
6 garlic cloves, coarsely chopped
2 cm (¾ in) piece ginger, coarsely chopped
2 brown onions, coarsely chopped
2 tablespoons ghee
1–2 sprigs curry leaves
1 lemongrass stalk, coarsely chopped
5 cardamom pods
1 cinnamon stick
2 tablespoons tamarind paste
Juice of ½ lemon
Brown sugar, to taste
Steamed rice, fried curry leaves and lime wedges, to serve

Rub beef with curry powder and chilli until nicely coated. Refrigerate for at least 2 hours or overnight to marinate.

Add garlic and ginger to a food processor and process until combined. Add onion and pulse to a coarse paste; you don't want to process it to a mush.

Heat ghee in a large heavy-based frying pan over medium heat. Add curry leaves, lemongrass, cardamom and cinnamon and fry, stirring occasionally, for 3–5 minutes until fragrant. Add onion mixture and cook, stirring occasionally, for 10–15 minutes until soft and golden, and the oil begins to separate at the bottom of the pan.

Increase heat to high, add beef and fry, turning occasionally for 5–10 minutes until browned, well-coated and catching on the bottom of the pan. Add tamarind paste, 1 teaspoon salt and enough water to cover the beef. Reduce heat to low and simmer for 1–1½ hours or until tender.

Add lemon juice and season with salt and sugar to taste — a little sugar can balance the flavours but this shouldn't be a sweet curry. Serve with rice, fried curry leaves and lime wedges.

Simon says slow-roasted citrus duck

Simon Marnie is a Sydney ABC radio host who regularly suffers our waffling on the Providores' Report section of his weekend show. A few days after he bought a pasture-raised, Aylesbury-Pekin duck from us, we received a fevered text raving about how he'd slow-roasted the duck using this brilliant new recipe featuring cumquats and mandarins, and said it was fantastic. Apparently his lunch guest, a successful Sydney restaurateur, got stuck in and had seconds and thirds and fourths. Simon was also squeaking with excitement about the rendered duck fat he had left over at the end, to use for roasting potatoes and carrots. We tried his recipe using some mandarins we had to hand and he was right: it was delicious.

Simon Marnie, retail customer

———

Feeds: 6, depending on the size of the duck and the appetite of your guests
Preparation time: 10 minutes | Cooking time: 7 hours
Special equipment: A roasting tin with a trivet or wire rack

1 large (2–2.25 kg/4 lb 8 oz–5 lb)
   pasture-raised duck, at room temperature
6 mandarins, cut in half
6 cumquats, cut in half
Olive oil, for drizzling

Preheat oven to 120°C (235°F). Score the breasts and fat of the duck, being careful not to pierce the flesh.

Stuff the cavity with cumquats and mandarins; the sweet juices and the intense flavour of the skins will release into the duck as it cooks. If you're finicky, you can seal the cavity with toothpicks.

Rub duck skin with a little olive oil and salt it liberally. Place duck on a trivet or a wire rack in a roasting tin; this allows the fat to drain.

Roast for 7 hours until the skin is golden and crisp and the meat comes away from the bone easily. Serve with the roasted fruit (the fruit is also great blended into a sauce).

While the roasting tin is still warm, drain off the fat and strain it into jars. It can be stored in the fridge and used for baking, frying or roasting potatoes.

Ben and Reagan's beef short ribs with pickled carrots and noodles

'Ben and I moved to Sydney's inner west seven years ago, from Savannah, Georgia in the US. Since we arrived, our access to fresh produce has completely changed the way we think about food. In many ways our adventure started at Feather and Bone — the idea that what you put in your mouth should have a loving story that will carry over into the experience you share with your friends and family. This noodle bowl is a mesh of some of our favourite flavours from both our time here and abroad.'

Ben and Reagan Waring, retail customers

———

Feeds: 4–6 | Preparation time: 20 minutes | Cooking time: 3 hours 15 minutes

1 kg (2 lb 4 oz) beef short ribs,
  at room temperature
2 tablespoons olive oil
80 ml (2½ fl oz/⅓ cup) mirin
200 g (7 oz/¾ cup) white (shiro) miso
noodles of your choice (we like soba or
  ramen noodles), to serve
Sesame oil, chilli oil and soy sauce, to taste
Toppings of your choice (we like enoki
  mushrooms and shredded cabbage)
Sesame seeds, coriander (cilantro) leaves
  and lime wedges, to serve

Quick pickled carrots

4 carrots, cut into julienne
2 teaspoons finely diced ginger
4 garlic cloves
1 small red chilli
250 ml (9 fl oz/1 cup) apple cider
  vinegar (or enough to cover the
  vegetables in a bowl)
1½ teaspoons sugar
1½ teaspoons salt

Preheat oven to 120°C (235°F). Coat ribs with olive oil and season with salt and freshly ground black pepper. Heat a large frying pan over medium–high heat, add ribs and sear them, turning, for 10 minutes or until nicely browned on all sides. Remove from heat.

Stir mirin and miso in a bowl to combine, brush all over ribs, then place in a roasting tin and roast for 3 hours or until beef is tender and falling away from the bone.

Meanwhile, to make the pickles, place carrot in a heatproof bowl. Combine remaining ingredients with 125 ml (4 fl oz/½ cup) water in a small saucepan over medium heat and stir until salt and sugar dissolve. Pour pickling liquid over the carrots and cool to room temperature. They're ready to eat straight away, but will keep refrigerated in a clean jar for up to 2 weeks.

When ready to serve, cook noodles in a large saucepan of boiling water until al dente — they should still have elasticity. Drain, rinse under cold running water to stop them from cooking, drain again and toss with a little sesame oil to stop them sticking.

Divide noodles among bowls, toss with chilli oil and soy sauce to taste, add beef (Ben likes his short rib whole; I like mine sliced) and layer over toppings — you can layer the bowl with your favourite toppings or whatever you have to hand. Top with sesame seeds and coriander and serve with lime wedges.

David's Hungarian roast duck with seasonal fruit

'My mother's family fled Hungary and arrived in Australia with nothing in 1949, settling in Sydney's outer western suburbs where I was born. One of Mum's sisters raised geese and ducks in the backyard to be eaten for special occasions and Mum carried out the dispatching of the poultry, de-feathering the birds via the application of hot water. As a kid I was always keen to attend these events — much less so my father who, despite his large stature and generally silent demeanour, was a very gentle soul. I learnt to cook from Mum and it's been a welcome foil to the stress in my legal career, not to mention the great pleasure I get from feeding my family. This recipe is adapted from a Hungarian dish my mother used to make and that my family love. She'd probably roll her eyes if she could see what I've done to it, but I think she'd like it if she could taste it.'

David Cross, retail customer

———

Feeds: 4 | Preparation time: 15 minutes | Cooking time: 3 hours
Special equipment: Wire rack on a roasting tin, kitchen string

1 pasture-raised duck
  (2–2.5 kg/4 lb 8 oz–5 lb 8 oz)
2–3 seasonal citrus fruits (oranges, mandarins, clementines or a mix), thickly sliced
4 garlic cloves, thickly sliced
125 ml (4 fl oz/½ cup) juice from the chosen citrus
3 tablespoons balsamic vinegar
2 tablespoons honey

Preheat oven to 160°C (315°F).

Rinse duck under running water and thoroughly pat dry with paper towel. Lightly score breasts in parallel diagonal lines with a sharp knife — be careful not to cut through to the flesh. Stuff the cavity with citrus and garlic. Tie the legs together with kitchen string and secure the cavity with toothpicks or half a skewer.

Combine citrus juice and vinegar in a bowl. Set aside about 3 tablespoons of this mixture for the last stage.

Rub the duck all over with salt and place breast-side up on a wire rack in a roasting tin. Roast for 1 hour, then carefully turn duck over and roast for 40 minutes, breast-side down. Turn duck back over and baste with some citrus and vinegar mixture. Roast, basting every 10 minutes, for another 40 minutes.

Stir honey through reserved basting liquid until thoroughly combined. Remove duck from oven and brush all over with the honey mixture, then roast, brushing every 10 minutes, for a final 40 minutes until glossy, golden and cooked through. Rest for 5–10 minutes before carving.

Vince's slow-roasted lamb shoulder with paprika and honey

'I'm the sixth generation to farm our land at Moorlands, near Dalton, NSW and the first to farm biodynamically. We grow award-winning Texel sheep that we've been selling to Feather and Bone since 2011.

This is a foolproof dish, inspired by a recipe in Greg and Lucy Malouf's book *Moorish*, which I've cooked for as long as I can remember. The original recipe uses boned, diced lamb but I love the texture and depth of flavour the shoulder gives to this dish, with the marrow and connective tissue softening into a rich, layered, gelatinous sauce. You just pop it in the oven in the morning before you head off round the farm, check it at morning tea and it's ready in the afternoon.'

Vince Heffernan, producer

———

Feeds: 8 | Preparation time: 15 minutes | Cooking time: At least 7 hours
Equipment: A large, cast-iron saucepan that will hold a whole lamb shoulder

2–2.2 kg (4 lb 8 oz–5 lb) square-cut lamb shoulder on the bone
1 tablespoon olive oil
2 large brown onions, diced
3 garlic cloves, coarsely chopped
1 teaspoon sweet paprika
Finely grated zest and juice of 2 lemons
1 tablespoon honey
800 g (1 lb 12 oz) tomatoes, harvested in season and frozen (or use tinned)
1 cinnamon stick
1 handful herbs from the garden (mint, rosemary, thyme, flat-leaf parsley, oregano)
1–1.5 litres (35–52 fl oz/4–6 cups) chicken stock or water
500 g (1 lb 2 oz) dried risoni or orzo pasta
2 red chillies (optional), coarsely chopped
Grilled haloumi, lemon wedges, crusty bread and a green salad, to serve

Preheat oven to 100°C (225°F). Season lamb shoulder with salt and freshly ground black pepper.

Heat olive oil in a large cast-iron saucepan over medium heat, add onion and garlic and cook gently, stirring occasionally, for 5 minutes until softened. Add paprika, lemon zest and honey, and stir to coat. Place seasoned lamb shoulder on top and add tomatoes, cinnamon, lemon juice, herbs and 500 ml (17 fl oz/ 2 cups) of stock or water. Bring to the boil.

Put lid on and pop it on the bottom shelf of the oven. Let it gently cook for an hour or so, allowing the lamb to release some juices and fat. Take saucepan out of the oven to check and add the rest of the stock or water, pop it back in and leave it for another 6 hours or so.

Half an hour before you're planning to eat, take pan out, and add risoni or orzo and mix well. Return pan to the oven for another 25 minutes or until the pasta is cooked.

Serve with grilled haloumi dressed with a squeeze of lemon juice, fresh crusty bread and a crisp green salad.

Rachel's Oaxacan-style braised goat

'I discovered the rich, nourishing deliciousness of goat in the markets of Oaxaca, Mexico. Women line a modest hall, perched above simmering cauldrons filled with fragrant, goaty goodness, ladling out bowlfuls for their customers at communal tables while men with guitars stroll around serenading everyone! It was the very first dish on the menu when I opened my restaurant, Hearth & Soul.'

Rachel Jelly, chef and retail customer

———

Feeds: 6–8 | Preparation time: 25 minutes, plus soaking and marinating
Cooking time: 3–4 hours

1 pasture-raised goat shoulder
   (about 2–2.5 kg/4 lb 8 oz–5 lb 8 oz)
1.5 litres (3 lb 5 oz/6 cups) pasture-raised
   chicken stock
Juice of 1 orange
4 banana leaves (optional)
Juice of 1–2 limes
Tortillas, to serve

Marinade

4–6 pasilla chillies (available online, or
   substitute ancho chillies)
6 garlic cloves
½ brown onion
1 handful thyme sprigs, leaves picked
3 tablespoons apple cider vinegar
½ teaspoon cumin seeds
½ teaspoon cloves
8 allspice berries

To make the marinade, heat a frying pan over medium heat, add chillies and dry-fry, turning occasionally, for 5 minutes or until coloured but not blackened. Transfer to a heatproof bowl and cover with boiling water. Cover with a plate and leave to soak for 20 minutes. Drain, remove stalks and seeds and place the flesh in a small food processor or a mortar. Add remaining marinade ingredients, salt to taste and a little water (just to help it blend), and process or grind with a pestle until reasonably thick. Massage the marinade into the goat shoulder and leave it in the fridge overnight to marinate.

The next day, preheat oven to 170°C (325°F). Place goat shoulder in a large roasting tin or casserole with a lid. Bring chicken stock to the boil in a saucepan, then pour it around the shoulder, and add orange juice. The liquid should come about one-third of the way up the shoulder; add some boiling water to top up if necessary.

Cover goat shoulder with banana leaves, tucking them gently under the shoulder to hold them in place, or use baking paper. Roast for 3–4 hours until meat is pulling away from the bone. Remove from oven, cool, then remove meat from the bone and shred it into large pieces with two forks.

Pour the braising liquid into a saucepan and bring it to the boil. Add goat meat back in and stir for 5 minutes or until warmed through. Squeeze in lime juice to taste (I like mine very zesty), and adjust the seasoning to taste with salt and freshly ground black pepper.

Pile the goat into serving bowls, ladle the broth over and serve with tortillas. Save the bones to make goat stock, and use instead of the chicken stock the next time you make the dish.

Tammi's crispy pig's ear banh mi

'When we first started selling our pastured pork, I had only been eating meat for about seven years, after a decade of vegetarianism, and was determined to make use of every part of the animals we raise with such care. And so my crispy pig's ear banh mi was born, of necessity and respect, inspired by regular visits to Vietnam over the years. Banh mi are best when there is a balance of fat, fresh, sweet, sour, salt and spice, all wrapped up in a crispy baguette with a soft centre. These crispy pig's ear banh mi capture that formula perfectly, and also leave room for everyone at the table to self-determine their own ratios of each constituent flavour.'

Tammi Jonas, producer and activist

———

Feeds: 4–6 | Preparation time: 15 minutes, plus chilling | Cooking time: 8 hours

4 pasture-raised pigs' ears
1 leek, coarsely chopped
3 garlic cloves, lightly crushed, still in skin
50 g (1¾ oz) palm sugar
300 ml (10½ fl oz) pasture-raised pork
  bone broth or chicken stock
200 ml (7 fl oz) Shaoxing rice wine
200 ml (7 fl oz) soy sauce
6 star anise
1 cinnamon stick
3 eggs
Plain (all-purpose) flour, for dusting
60 g (2¼ oz/1 cup) panko breadcrumbs
Lard or rendered animal fat
  (see recipe on p144), for deep-frying
Crusty baguette or white rolls, to serve

Fillings

4–6 fried eggs
Freshly made mayonnaise or aïoli, to serve
40 g (¾ cup) lightly pickled carrot
2 cucumbers, cut into batons
Long red chilli, coarsely chopped, to taste
Coriander (cilantro) leaves, to serve
Fish sauce, to serve

Start this recipe 1–2 days ahead. Preheat oven to 120°C (235°F). Place pigs' ears in an ovenproof dish with leek, garlic, sugar, broth or stock, Shaoxing, soy sauce and spices. Cover with baking paper, seal tightly with foil, and braise for about 8 hours, or overnight, until very tender.

Place ears on a cooling rack in the fridge to dry out for up to 1 day.

Slice ears into thin strips. Beat eggs in a wide bowl and place flour and breadcrumbs in separate bowls. Dust pigs' ears in flour, shaking off excess, dip in egg, then coat in breadcrumbs. Melt 5 cm (2 in) fat in a deep, heavy-based saucepan until shimmering, then deep-fry ears for 2–3 minutes until crisp and golden. Remove with a slotted spoon and drain on a wire rack.

Serve pigs' ears in baguettes or rolls, and offer fried eggs, mayonnaise, pickled carrot, cucumber, chilli, coriander and fish sauce for people to fill as they like. Voilà — a crunchy, salty, sweet, sour, spicy banh mi made with a part of the pig most people wouldn't know what to do with. Uncommonly delicious.

Dan's peposo

'Peposo is a rich, heavily peppered beef stew from Tuscany, made with the local red wine. At Don Peppino's we finish it with crispy lardons to make it even more banging and delicious. Any succulent piece of braising beef will work. We use a combo of beef neck/chuck and rib or short rib meat.'

Dan Johnstone, chef and restaurateur

———

Feeds: 10–12 | Preparation time: 20 minutes, plus marinating | Cooking time: 3½ hours

1 kg (2 lb 4 oz) boneless beef neck, cut into large cubes

1 kg (2 lb 4 oz) boneless short rib, cut into large cubes

40 g (1½ oz) freshly ground black pepper, plus extra to serve

110 ml (3¾ fl oz) olive oil

2 brown onions, thinly sliced

2 carrots, sliced

2 celery stalks, sliced

250 g (9 oz) button mushrooms, sliced

100 g (3½ oz) tomato paste

1 litre (35 fl oz/4 cups) red wine

6 thyme sprigs

1 litre (35 fl oz/4 cups) chicken stock

200 g (7 oz) guanciale (available from select delicatessens), cut into lardons about the size of a pinkie finger

Place beef in a large bowl and cover with pepper — more than you think is healthy — and some salt. Marinate in the fridge for 1 hour.

Preheat oven to 150°C (300°F).

Heat 2 tablespoons olive oil in a large, deep-sided frying pan over medium–high heat. Add onion, carrot and celery, and sauté for about 10 minutes, getting some nice deep, golden-brown colour action. Reduce heat to low and cook, stirring occasionally, for a further 10 minutes or until soft and sweet.

Heat 1 tablespoon oil in a frying pan over high heat and sauté mushrooms for 2–3 minutes until golden. Add mushrooms to vegetables and add tomato paste. Cook, stirring, for 2–3 minutes, then add wine and bring to the boil. Reduce heat to medium and simmer for 10 minutes or until wine is reduced by about half.

Meanwhile, heat 2 tablespoons oil in a separate large frying pan over high heat. Sear beef in batches, turning, for 5–10 minutes or until deeply browned on all sides, taking care not to overcrowd the pan, and transferring each batch to a large roasting tin or casserole dish.

Pour vegetable and wine mixture over the beef, and add enough chicken stock to just cover. Cover tightly with a lid or foil, place in the oven and cook for about 3 hours, checking occasionally. You want the meat tender and soft but not completely falling apart.

Add guanciale to a small cold frying pan with 2 teaspoons oil. Cook over low heat, stirring occasionally, for 20 minutes or until fat renders and guanciale is crisp and golden. Drain on paper towel.

When beef is ready, lift the meat out of the pan. Strain the braising liquor through a fine strainer, season to taste, then pour the liquor back over the meat. Stir in the guanciale and serve.

Leah's healing bone broth

'When one's immune and digestive systems aren't optimal, bone broth rich in collagen and immune-stimulating properties are vital to heal the digestive system to assist in absorption of nutrients. Clinically, I find chicken bone broth — especially from Sommerlad chickens — is my number one strategy for patients to heal their digestive system and repair their body on the path to wellness. If they're recovering from an infection, depleted, burnt out or have systemic inflammation, it's my go-to food. Couple this with some slow-cooked lamb, ghee, and mild ingredients, and it's one of the gentlest and most rebuilding recipes I give my patients.'

Leah Hechtman, retail customer

———

Feeds: 4–6 | Preparation time: 15 minutes | Cooking time: 18–24 hours
Special equipment: A large stainless steel saucepan — slow-cookers, pressure-cookers or enamel pots do not extract the same fat and collagen content from the carcasses

2–3 Sommerlad chicken carcasses with legs (optional), skin removed
Pure spring or filtered water

Place carcasses in a large saucepan and cover with water. Bring to a simmer, reduce heat to as low as it will go, and simmer, skimming any scum that rises to the surface, for 18–24 hours until there's a glossy sheen on top.

Remove carcasses, then strain broth through a fine sieve. When cooled it should be a gelatinous texture. (Do not remove the white fat layer — this is the most important part of the broth.) Store in small glass containers and refrigerate or freeze to use as needed. Broth will keep refrigerated for up to 3 days or frozen for 3 months.

Kefalonia meat pie à la Persefoni

'Diversity is the spice of life and spices make for diverse food. The Greek recipes I learnt from my mum, aunties and others really warm my heart. This one is from my cousin — it's a very traditional dish from our island of Kefalonia. Hope you enjoy it!'

Sue Thliveris, retail customer

———

Feeds: 6–8 | Preparation time: 40 minutes, plus resting and cooling
Cooking time: 1 hour to 1 hour 10 minutes

250 ml (9 fl oz/1 cup) olive oil
500 g (1 lb 2 oz) blade or chuck steak, cut into bite-sized pieces
500 g (1 lb 2 oz) pork neck, cut into bite-sized pieces
1 brown onion, coarsely chopped
2 garlic cloves, coarsely chopped
1 handful flat-leaf parsley, coarsely chopped
1 ripe tomato, seeds removed, grated (discard skin)
2–3 tablespoons tomato paste
½ teaspoon nutmeg
5 cloves
½ teaspoon ground cinnamon
½ teaspoon dried Greek oregano
½ teaspoon dried marjoram
200 g arborio or other short-grain rice
125 g Swiss Brown or button mushrooms, thickly sliced or quartered
1 zucchini (courgette), coarsely chopped
80–100 g (2¾ oz–3½ oz) kefalotiri (from select supermarkets and Greek delis), cut into 2 cm (¾ in) dice

Pastry

600 g (1 lb 5 oz) plain (all-purpose) flour
200 ml (7 fl oz) olive oil
1 tablespoon white wine or vinegar

Heat 1 tablespoon olive oil in a large, heavy-based saucepan over medium–high heat. Cook meat in batches for 5–7 minutes until browned all over, adding a little more oil for each batch. Return all meat to the pan, reduce heat to medium, add onion and garlic and cook, stirring occasionally, for 8–10 minutes or until light golden.

Add parsley, tomato and tomato paste and simmer for 5 minutes or until slightly thickened. Add spices and herbs and season with salt and pepper. Stir well, add any remaining oil and 250 ml (9 fl oz/1 cup) water, then bring to a simmer. Cover with a lid, reduce heat to low and cook for 40–45 minutes until meat is tender.

Add rice and simmer, stirring occasionally, for 6–8 minutes until par-cooked, then add mushroom and zucchini and cook, stirring, for a few more minutes until rice is cooked and vegetables are tender. Cool to room temperature, then stir in the kefalotiri. Cool completely.

To make the pastry, combine flour, 1 teaspoon salt, 280 ml warm water, olive oil and vinegar in a bowl. Stir with a fork until dough comes together, adding a little more water if needed, then transfer to a lightly floured surface and knead briefly until smooth. Wrap in plastic wrap and refrigerate for 1 hour (or up to 1–2 days) to rest.

Preheat oven to 180°C (350°F). Cut pastry in half. Roll out one half on a lightly floured surface until 3–4 (⅛ in) mm thick and use it to line a 28 cm (11 in) tart tin or baking dish. Add filling. Roll out remaining pastry and place on top, trimming excess and pinching edges together to seal. Make an incision in the top to allow the steam to escape. Bake for 60–70 minutes until crisp and golden — cover top with foil if it's browning too quickly. Cool briefly before serving.

Laura's grandma's Cornish pasties

'My grandmother was a true Cornish woman, famed for her pasties. I remember her hands lightly pinching and folding the pastry to seal the edges. Crimping is something of an art form, born of practical origins. In the old days, pasties were a favourite lunchtime meal for workers in Cornwall's many coal and tin mines. The hungry men would hold their lunch by its crimped edge, eat their delicious pasty, and simply discard the crust they'd been holding in their dirty hands. I've replaced some of the lard with butter, but the recipe is otherwise authentic.'

Laura Bishop, retail customer

———

Makes: 4 large pasties (kids normally eat half each) | Preparation time: 35 minutes
Cooking time: 1 hour

125 g (4½ oz) butter
125 g (4½ oz/½ cup) lard
450 g (1 lb/3 cups) plain (all-purpose) flour
1 swede, cut into 3 cm (1¼ in) cubes, then thinly sliced
2 potatoes, cut into 3 cm (1¼ in) cubes, then thinly sliced
400 g (14 oz) skirt steak, cut into 1 cm (½ in) pieces
1 large brown onion, finely chopped
Milk, for brushing
Chutney, tomato sauce or HP sauce, to serve

Cut butter and lard into 2.5 cm (1 in) cubes and freeze for a few hours. Place in a food processor with flour and a pinch of salt and pulse until mixture resembles breadcrumbs, adding a spoonful or two of water to bring it together. (Alternatively, freeze the fats whole, then grate them into flour on a clean surface. Combine, then add water and chop together with a knife.) Shape into a fat disc, wrap in plastic wrap and refrigerate for 30 minutes.

Cut pastry into four. Shape one portion into a rough disc and roll it out to the thickness of a coin. Use a 22 cm (8½ in) plate to cut out a circle. Layer a quarter of swede and potato in the centre, season with salt and pepper, top with a quarter of the steak and onion, and season again. Pile it as high as possible, leaving a pastry border to make sealing easier. Dip a finger in water and run it around the edge, then fold pastry up around filling to form a half-moon shape, squeezing the edges together to roughly seal. Crimp pastry by folding over small sections of the edge, away from you, until completely sealed. Repeat with remaining pastry and filling.

Preheat oven to 200°C (400°F). Transfer pasties to a lined baking tray and brush with milk. Make a few small incisions in the centre to let the steam out. (Grandma always cut our initials, personalising each pasty.) Bake for 15 minutes, then reduce heat to 150°C (300°F) and bake for another 45 minutes until golden brown. Enjoy with lashings of chutney, tomato sauce or HP sauce.

Angie's humble pie

'I learnt to cook with my grandma. By the time I was born, she was virtually blind and cooked by experience, taste and feel — like any good country cook. I now teach women who have experienced trauma how to cook and enjoy food, and I also manage the Two Good Soup Kitchen, using Feather and Bone meat and organic vegetables to provide the best food to the people who need it most. This is my take on a humble pie, so-called because it uses the humblest of ingredients. I developed it when teaching offal classes at Feather and Bone, and it's an easy introduction to offal — kids love it drenched in tomato sauce. Adjust the flavours to your taste, but the idea is to tie the sweet spices with the richness of the offal.'

Angie Prendergast-Sceats, chef

———

Feeds: 6 | Preparation time: 30 minutes | Cooking time: 1 hour

Butter, for greasing
120 g (4¼ oz) each liver, heart and kidney (from a selection of animals or solely beef or lamb)
250 g (9 oz) minced beef or lamb
2 tablespoons beef suet (order from your butcher)
1 tablespoon plain (all-purpose) flour
1 brown onion, chopped
1 carrot, chopped
2 celery stalks, thinly sliced
2 garlic cloves, finely chopped
2 teaspoons quatre épices (from select grocers)
1 teaspoon fennel seeds
2 bay leaves
400 g (14 oz) tinned chopped tomatoes
2½ tablespoons balsamic vinegar
1 teaspoon dried oregano
2 tablespoons tomato paste
70 g (2½ oz/½ cup) currants or raisins
2 tablespoons capers
1 small handful flat-leaf parsley leaves, finely chopped
1 sheet ready-rolled puff pastry
1 pasture-raised egg, beaten
Mash and peas or a green salad, to serve

Preheat oven to 180°C (350°F). Butter a deep-sided 28 cm pie dish ready for filling. (Or use smaller dishes for individual pies.)

Trim any excess fat or sinew off liver, heart and kidneys and finely chop them together to form a coarse mince-like texture. Combine with minced meat, then combine thoroughly with beef suet.

Heat a large saucepan over medium heat, add meat mixture in batches and cook, stirring occasionally, for 5–10 minutes until browned. Transfer to a mixing bowl and lightly toss with flour.

Throw onion, carrot and celery into the saucepan and cook, stirring, for 5 minutes or until soft. Add garlic, stir for a further 2 minutes, then add spices and bay leaves and stir well to coat. Add tinned tomatoes, oregano, tomato paste and balsamic vinegar and season to taste with salt and freshly ground black pepper.

Return meat to the pan and stir well. Cook, stirring, over medium heat for 5 minutes or until combined and warmed through, then stir through currants, capers and parsley. Remove from heat to cool.

Place meat filling in the buttered pie dish and top with puff pastry sheet to cover. Trim excess pastry and pinch the edges to the side of the dish to seal. Brush the pie top with egg. With a sharp knife, make 2 small cuts in the pie top to let air escape.

Bake for 30 minutes or until pastry is golden and crisp. Serve immediately with mash and peas or a crisp green salad.

Danielle's lamb leg
'à la ficelle', page 218.

9.
You should do this

At least once

From Ye olde mincemeat pies and a pig's head terrine to a spit roasted lamb for 40.

Danielle's lamb leg 'à la ficelle'

'I'm a Cuban–American chef from Miami, USA and I arrived in Sydney in 2013 to set up Fred's, a Merivale restaurant that celebrates uncomplicated food made with great produce. The addictive pleasure I get from working with beautiful, sustainably produced ingredients made me a natural fit with Feather and Bone and we started doing things together a few years before my restaurant opened — they've been supplying us since then. This recipe has become a signature dish at Fred's, where we pretty much built a hearth to be able to cook lamb this way. It's totally primitive but absolute perfection.

A hanging leg of lamb hung "by a string" (hence the "à la ficelle" in French) in front of a fire. Gravity and radiant heat do their work to keep the leg spinning so that it gently roasts on all sides. A high-quality whole leg of lamb is essential here as it is such a pure expression of the meat. You don't entirely need a hearth to cook this way and any open fireplace or fire pit will surely accommodate, if you get a little creative with your setup. Whatever setup you cobble together, being able to trap the heat and reflect it onto the leg will help to speed the process. Metal plates or bricks will do the job but if a lot of heat is lost to the sides or top, it may extend the cooking time to 2½ hours. The leg itself can be suspended from an improvised tripod constructed from some star pickets held together by a twist of wire.

Ask your butcher for a whole leg of lamb, and I mean entirely whole with ankle tendon still attached (this is where you will hang it from). You can ask your butcher to help you prepare the lamb leg by removing the aitch bone. You can also ask them to tunnel-bone out the femur but it's not essential, it just makes it easier to carve once cooked.'

Danielle Alvarez, chef and retail customer

———

Feeds: 6–8 | Preparation time: 15 minutes, plus 6 hours (or overnight) to marinate
Cooking time: 1.5–2 hours | Special equipment: A hearth or firepit with somewhere to hang a lamb leg, kitchen string and a thermometer

5 garlic cloves
½ bunch rosemary, leaves picked and
  finely chopped
1 bunch thyme, leaves picked and
  finely chopped
3 tablespoons olive oil
1 whole leg of lamb (about 3–4 kg/6 lb 12 oz
–8 lb 13 oz), with ankle tendon still
  attached (order from your butcher)
Roasted potatoes, a green salad,
  lemon wedges and a fresh, green olive
  oil, to serve

Crush garlic with a mortar and pestle and combine with herbs and olive oil. Rub this marinade all around the outside and the inside cavity of the lamb leg (if it has been tunnel-boned), then season it liberally with salt and freshly ground black pepper. If the leg has been boned, tie it up with kitchen string to make it as even as possible — a few ties that fold the bottom flap up and a tie near the tendon are good, as well as 3 or 4 ties around the meaty part of the leg to keep everything roughly the same size. Tie a loop securely around the ankle with about 20 cm (8 in) extra string — this is where you'll hang it from. Refrigerate for at least 6 hours or overnight to allow the seasoning to penetrate.

Bring lamb to room temperature for about 1 hour before cooking. Start a fire in the fireplace and decide on a place where you can hang the leg, where it will be spinning approximately 20 cm (8 in) from the flames and 5–10 cm (2–4 in) off the ground (place a dish underneath to catch the drippings — some par-boiled potatoes in here would also be delicious). Hang the leg so it is dangling by the looped string and give a spin. Gravity and heat should keep it spinning gently but you may need to give it a nudge every now and then.

Once lamb is browned, start checking the internal temperature. For medium, you want the thermometer to read about 65°C (150°F). Once the desired temperature is reached, cut the leg down and let it rest for at least 15 minutes.

Carve and serve with roasted potatoes, a salad, a few wedges of lemon and fresh green olive oil.

Keita's tsukune

Keita has been a long-term customer of Feather and Bone, initially as a private retail customer nurturing a dream to open a restaurant in Sydney, and then when he did open his restaurants to considerable acclaim, as a wholesale customer. Yakitori is his specialty, and tsukune is a Japanese chicken meatball, often cooked on a skewer.

Keita Abe, chef and retail customer

———

Feeds: 4 | Preparation time: 15 minutes | Cooking time: 45 minutes
Special equipment: Thermometer, wooden skewers, barbecue or charcoal grill

5 eggs
75 g (2¾ oz) organic or pasture-raised chicken thigh, minced (ask your butcher to do this)
125 g (4½ oz) chicken cartilage from the front of the breast bone, finely diced (ask your butcher to do this)
100 g (3½ oz) pasture-raised pork belly, minced (ask your butcher to do this)
1 spring onion (scallion), finely diced
1 cm (½ in) piece ginger, finely grated
2 garlic cloves, finely grated
½ teaspoon ground coriander (cilantro)
1 tablespoon potato starch or cornflour
Shichimi togarashi (from Asian grocers) and sauce of your choice (such as teriyaki or tare), to serve

To make 'ontama' eggs, cook 4 eggs in a saucepan of water at 68°C (150°F) for 30 minutes. Drain, and leave to come back to room temperature before gently cracking into a bowl.

Add minced chicken thigh, diced cartilage and minced pork belly to a bowl with spring onion, garlic, coriander, potato starch or cornflour, the remaining egg and a pinch of salt. Mix gently and evenly until you get a smooth mixture.

Using your hands, mould a palmful of the mince into an oblong shape and skewer lengthways with one or two skewers per piece. Repeat with remaining mince.

Preheat a charcoal grill or barbecue to medium–high. Place skewers on the grill and cook, turning often, for 10–15 minutes until a nice golden colour is achieved and mince is cooked through.

Serve immediately with cracked ontama eggs, shichimi togarashi and your favourite sauce.

James' luxe Mud burgers

'This is a special treat I make twice a year for the Mud Studio team. There's 40 of us here so it's always a little stressful as everything is in the timing and I come out the other side with an even deeper respect for short-order cooks. The inspiration comes from a fabulous haché-style burger ("le casti burger", pronounced "burr-jer") served at La Castiglione, a very red, very comfy bistro on the Right Bank in Paris, which has become a ritual for us when we just happen to be that-a-way. It's just a burger, but the aim is to make it as premium and luxurious as possible, so buy the best meat and vegetables you can find and take as much care as you can in preparation and you'll have something special. We do have some vegetarians at Mud so for them we swap the patty for a large field mushroom, sautéed in garlic, thyme and butter.

With the patties, you're aiming for a very coarse mince similar to a French steak haché. You can use a grinder on the coarsest setting, or hand-cut it as finely as possible. If you hand-cut, it should look like a coarse mince and take longer than seems reasonable. Ideally you'll have about 25 per cent fat in the mix. Most of the fat will come from the brisket and short rib. Use your eye to guesstimate the fat percentage and err on the side of too fatty. Alternatively, ask your butcher to grind the beef for you and roll it into a log to cut patties from — but make sure to give instructions on the coarseness and fat percentage, and don't let them talk you out of the blend.'

James Kirton, retail customer

———

Feeds: 8–10 | Preparation time: 2 hours, plus resting | Cooking time: 10 minutes
Special equipment: Barbecue with a grill and a hotplate. It's also best to have an assistant — timing is everything and things get a bit heated at the pointy end.

500 g (1 lb 2 oz) sirloin, minced

500 g (1 lb 2 oz) brisket, minced

500 g (1 lb 2 oz) short rib (bone out), minced

1 white onion, finely diced

2 tablespoons mirin

8 milk buns or brioche buns, cut in half and buttered

4 ripe beefsteak tomatoes, thickly cut

1 iceberg lettuce, leaves separated and broken into bun-sized pieces

Dijon mustard, to taste

Large dill pickles, to serve

Potato chips and tomato sauce, to serve

Special sauce

1 teaspoon garlic flakes

1 teaspoon smoked paprika

2 teaspoons Dijon mustard

1 tablespoon tomato paste

4 tablespoons pickle brine

120 g (4¼ oz/½ cup) whole-egg mayonnaise

Cheese sauce

15 g (½ oz) butter

1 tablespoon plain (all-purpose) flour

150 ml (5 fl oz) milk

75 g (2¾ oz/¾ cup) grated emmental

75 g (2¾ oz/¾ cup) grated cheddar

2 thyme sprigs

Season all the minced beef with salt and freshly ground black pepper and toss it all together with two forks. Spread on a tray lined with baking paper and refrigerate, uncovered, overnight to dry out the meat. If you have the time, toss mince every six hours or so to expose as much of the mince to the air as possible.

To make the special sauce, combine all ingredients in a jar. You're aiming for a tomato sauce-like consistency — if it's too thick, thin it with extra pickle juice; if it's too thin, add more mayonnaise. Taste and adjust accordingly. It should be equally creamy, spicy and tangy. Refrigerate overnight to allow the flavours to meld.

To make the cheese sauce, melt butter in a saucepan over medium heat, stir in flour and cook, stirring, for 3–5 minutes until sand-coloured. Whisking constantly, slowly add milk until smooth, then remove from heat, add cheese and thyme, and whisk until melted and combined. Transfer to a bowl and refrigerate until needed.

When ready to cook, gently shape each patty by hand, not too tightly, and chill in the refrigerator for 30 minutes; you want the meat as cold as possible prior to hitting the grill. Just before grilling, season the patties again with salt and pepper.

Toss onion with mirin in a bowl. Heat a barbecue grill and hotplate to high. Place seasoned patties on the grill and press down with a spatula — you want sizzle and smoke but not flame. Grill for 3 minutes, then flip, press down with a spatula and top each patty with a heaped teaspoon of mirin-soaked onion and a tablespoon of cheese sauce. The patties might be falling apart a little; use the spatula to keep them together.

Meanwhile, toast the buns on the hotplate, outside first, then inside, for 30 seconds to 1 minute each side or until lightly toasted. When done, pass the buns to an assistant to plate. (Your assistant can, if desired, add mustard to the base of the bun at this point.)

Cook patties for a further 2 minutes for medium–rare, then transfer them to toasted buns. Top each patty with a spoonful of special sauce, one tomato slice and a few leaves of lettuce and transfer to plates. Serve with a pickle and the top of the bun on the side. At Mud we also serve the burgers with the best potato chips we can get, along with extra tomato sauce, pickles and mustard on the table, plus soft drinks, beers or a medium-bodied red.

Jeremy's corned beef with white sauce and suet dumplings

This recipe is a combination of two of Jeremy Strode's corned beef recipes, kindly supplied by Jane Strode, with some elements from our own pickling recipe for corned beef. Some of the ingredients we would use in the pickle, Jeremy uses in the poaching broth, so this represents something of a joint effort. You'll also find a recipe for the traditional accompaniment of white sauce and one for suet dumplings as well.

I asked Jane for this recipe because Jeremy Strode was the very first customer of Feather and Bone. He bought one of three whole Southdown lambs that made up our first consignment. He would later buy many Wiltshire Horn lambs from us and they were his favourite. I think he was particularly chuffed that he could source lamb bearing the name of his home patch in England.

It's been said many times before but Jeremy is sorely missed by many in the Australian food world. He was a friend to Feather and Bone and we're delighted to include this recipe here.

Jeremy Strode, chef

———

Feeds: 4–6 | Preparation time: 30 minutes, plus brining, cooling | Cooking time: 3 hours

1–1.5 kg (2 lb 4 oz–3 lb 5 oz) piece
   silverside or whole eye of silverside
   (beef girello)
1 carrot
1 brown onion, cut in half
1 celery stalk
6 garlic cloves
1 bay leaf
3 thyme sprigs
12 black peppercorns
3 star anise
1 clove
1 teaspoon coriander seeds
Boiled potatoes and a green salad, to serve

Beef pickle

300 g (10½ oz/2¼ cups) sea salt
200 g (7 oz) caster sugar
2 bay leaves
6 cloves
6 black peppercorns
6 juniper berries
2 teaspoons celery seeds
1 teaspoon yellow mustard seeds

Suet dumplings

60 g (2¼ oz) suet (order from
   your butcher)
125 g (4½ oz) plain (all-purpose) flour
2 teaspoons salt
½ teaspoon baking powder

White sauce

50 g (1¾ oz) butter
50 g (1¾ oz/⅓ cup) plain (all-purpose) flour
1 litre (35 fl oz/4 cups) strained beef
   cooking liquor
1 tablespoon Dijon mustard
1 tablespoon fresh grated horseradish
   (use a good-quality jarred horseradish if
   you can't find fresh)
2 tablespoons pouring cream

To make the beef pickle, combine salt, sugar, bay leaves and spices in a large saucepan, add 2 litres (68 fl oz/8 cups) water and bring to the boil. Cool to room temperature. Submerge beef in the brine, cover, and refrigerate for 1 week.

To cook the beef, combine carrot, onion, celery, garlic, bay leaf, thyme, peppercorns, star anise, clove and coriander seeds in a large saucepan. Add 3 litres (101 fl oz/12 cups) water, bring to the boil, then add pickled beef and return to the boil. Reduce heat to low and simmer gently for 2–2½ hours or until tender (test with a skewer). Remove from heat and cool in liquor.

Meanwhile, to make the suet dumplings, combine all ingredients in a bowl and mix slowly with cold water (add just a little at a time) until a dough is formed. Roll dough into a cylinder on a lightly floured surface, cut into 6 pieces and roll each piece into a ball. While beef is cooking, gently poach dumplings in corned beef liquor for 20 minutes, or do it separately at the end.

While beef is cooling, make the white sauce. Melt butter in a saucepan over low heat. Add flour and cook, stirring continuously, for 10 minutes. Slowly whisk in 1 litre (35 fl oz) strained cooking liquor and cook over low heat, stirring occasionally, for 20 minutes or until thickened and smooth. Pass sauce through a fine sieve.

Reheat remaining cooking liquor in a saucepan over medium heat, and cut beef into 2–3 slices per serve. Gently warm the beef in the liquor. Reheat 500 ml (17 fl oz/2 cups) white sauce, add mustard, horseradish and a dash of cream. Season with salt and freshly ground white pepper to taste. Divide beef among warm plates and pour sauce over meat. Serve with suet dumplings or boiled potatoes, and a green salad.

Note: White sauce and beef (in the remaining liquor) will keep refrigerated for up to 1 week.

Feather and Bone's jambon persillé

This is a simple and delicious way to use up the end of your Christmas ham and also earn nose-to-tail points by incorporating trotters into your cooking. Jambon persillé is easy to make and a delicious crowd-pleaser. As with many such dishes in France, there are many jambon recipes and whoever you talk to will be adamant that theirs is the best. Our version is based on one given to us by Angie Prendergast-Sceats, who teaches our secondary-cuts cooking classes and, naturally, we reckon it's the best.

———

Makes: 4 small jars or 1 small terrine | Preparation time: 10 minutes
Cooking time: 4–4½ hours | Special equipment: 4 small jars or 1 small terrine mould

3 smoked ham hocks
2 pig's trotters
100 ml (3½ fl oz) dry white wine
2 bunches flat-leaf parsley, coarsely
   chopped, 5 stalks reserved
6 black peppercorns
100 ml (3½ fl oz) Champagne vinegar
   (or any good-quality, high-acid vinegar)
Crusty bread and cornichons, to serve

Place ham hocks, trotters, white wine, parsley stalks and peppercorns in a large saucepan and cover with cold water. Bring to the boil, then reduce heat to low and simmer for 3–4 hours or until meat is falling off the bone. Remove hocks and trotters from the stock and cool briefly. Strain the stock and cool to room temperature.

When the meat is cool enough to handle, shred the meat from the bones into a large bowl, discarding all the fat, skin and bones. Add half the chopped parsley and half the vinegar, taste, and add more of both to suit your taste. Season the meat with salt and freshly ground black pepper to taste, keeping in mind this will be combined with the stock — adjust the seasoning as required.

Either fill small jars with the shredded, dressed meat or line a small terrine mould with plastic wrap and gently press the meat into it. Pour the stock over the meat and press the meat into the stock so the top is even. Cover with plastic wrap and refrigerate until firm — the stock should set into a lovely, firm jelly around the meat and parsley mix.

Serve in jars or sliced with fresh, crusty bread, cornichons or pickles and your favourite refreshing beverage.

Norman's lamb tongue with numbing chilli and tahini sauce

'This recipe is from northern China, where middle Asian and Arabian influences blend with the complex beauty of Sichuan cooking to shine brightly. It often uses sliced pork belly but I think lamb tongue, with its tender buttery texture, is much more luxurious. This recipe is also a good way to use up any leftover roast lamb.'

Norman Lee, retail customer

———

Feeds: 4–6 as a shared entree | Preparation time: 20 minutes
Cooking time: 2 hours | Special equipment: Pressure cooker (optional)

500 g (1 lb 2 oz) lamb's tongues
2 small star anise
2 cloves
½ cinnamon stick
1 tablespoon Sichuan peppercorns
3 bay leaves
1 tablespoon sunflower oil
Coarsely chopped coriander (cilantro)
  leaves, to serve
1 teaspoon toasted sesame seeds

Numbing chilli-oil vinaigrette

25 g (1 oz) crushed Sichuan peppercorns
100 ml (3½ fl oz) sunflower oil
2 tablespoons black (Chinkiang) vinegar
1 tablespoon chilli oil
  (I use Lao Gan Ma brand)
1 garlic clove, finely chopped

Tahini sauce

1 tablespoon tahini
1 tablespoon sesame oil
½ tablespoon light soy sauce

If you have a pressure cooker, fill it with the minimum amount of water, then add tongues, star anise, cloves, cinnamon, Sichuan pepper, bay leaves and 1 teaspoon salt. Heat until it comes to full pressure, cook for 5 minutes, allow to cool, then drain. Alternatively, add tongues, spices, bay leaves and salt to a large saucepan, add enough water just to cover, bring to the boil, skim surface, then reduce heat to medium–low and simmer gently for 2 hours or until just tender — a skewer should pass through with only a little resistance.

Cool tongues until cool enough to handle, then peel off the skin with a small knife while tongues are still warm. Slice tongues thinly lengthwise — you should get about 4 slices per tongue.

Meanwhile, to make vinaigrette, warm crushed Sichuan pepper in oil in a small saucepan over low heat for 3–5 minutes or until fragrant — be careful, it can burn quickly. Remove from heat and steep for 10 minutes to extract all the fragrance. Strain, discarding Sichuan pepper, and combine oil with remaining ingredients.

Whisk all tahini sauce ingredients with 3 tablespoons warm water until smooth and silky. Add more water if needed; sauce should be a pouring consistency. Season to taste with salt.

For a cold summer dish, arrange tongue on a plate. (For a warm dish, heat oil in a frying pan over medium–high heat, add tongues, and cook, turning halfway, for 3–5 minutes until crisp and golden.) To serve, spoon the tahini sauce over. Splash on the chilli-oil vinaigrette, pile chopped coriander in the middle, and sprinkle with toasted sesame seeds. Toss at the table and serve.

Norman's vitello lingua tonnato

'This dish is my nose-to-tail variation on vitello tonnato, that inexplicably wondrous cold Italian dish, which combines thin slices of veal (vitello) with tuna sauce (tonnato). Vitello tonnato typically uses veal girello, a very lean cut from the hind leg that is next to the veal nut and sometimes called eye of silverside. The girello is a tricky cut that needs careful poaching or cooking via sous vide to ensure slices are not overly dry. It was a "Eureka!" moment when I discovered beef or veal tongue is a more than desirable substitute. Tongue has an equally mild flavour but is also luxuriously tender and much more forgiving to prepare. Cooking tongue may seem intimidating but all you need is patience and a little care. As with many secondary cuts, a pressure cooker provides speed and efficiency.'

Norman Lee, retail customer

———

Feeds: 4–6 as antipasto | Preparation time: 20 minutes
Cooking time: 2–3 hours | Special equipment: Pressure cooker (optional)

1 large beef tongue (or 2 veal tongues)
1 carrot, unpeeled and coarsely chopped
1 celery stalk, coarsely chopped
2 cloves
1 star anise
2 bay leaves
1 lemon, very thinly sliced into rounds
1 teaspoon baby capers, rinsed
Flat-leaf parsley leaves, to serve

Tonnato sauce

250 g (9 oz) tinned tuna in oil
2 hard-boiled eggs
2 anchovy fillets
1 teaspoon baby capers, rinsed
3 tablespoons extra-virgin olive oil
Juice of ½ lemon
Freshly ground black pepper, to taste

If you have a pressure cooker, place tongue, vegetables, spices, bay and 1 tablespoon salt in pressure cooker and cover with water. Heat until full pressure, then cook for 35 minutes. Remove from heat and allow pressure to release naturally until the lid can be opened (about 1 hour). Alternatively, combine ingredients in a large saucepan with 1 tablespoon salt, add water to cover, bring to the boil, reduce heat to low and simmer for 2–3 hours or until a skewer can pass through the tongue with only a little resistance.

Remove tongue from the pressure cooker or saucepan, reserving 125 ml (½ cup) poaching liquor. Cool briefly, then, while still warm, use a small knife to peel off the thick skin on the outside of the tongue (start from the sides to make it easier). Slice the peeled tongue crossways into 5 mm (¼ in) slices (this is important), cutting at an angle to obtain larger slices.

Combine the tonnato sauce ingredients in a food processor or blender and process until smooth. Add a splash of warm poaching liquor and blend to the consistency of a thin mayonnaise.

Spread tongue slices on a platter. Spoon over a thick layer of tonnato sauce, leaving a border of tongue undressed. Serve topped with lemon slices, capers, parsley and freshly ground black pepper.

Elle and Alessandro's buffalo ricotta ravioli with sage and rosemary butter

'This recipe includes two fillings — buffalo ricotta and spinach, and ricotta and buffalo mince — served together with the herb butter. Exact quantities don't really exist in Italy but a rough guide for the dough is 100 g (3½ oz/⅔ cup) flour to 1 egg.'

Elizabeth Farr and Alessandro Pezzella, retail customers

———

Feeds: 6 | Preparation time: 2 hours | Cooking time: 10 minutes
Special equipment: A pasta roller or a rolling pin

1 bunch silverbeet (stalks trimmed) or spinach, coarsely chopped
2 tablespoons extra-virgin olive oil, plus extra to serve
2 garlic cloves, 1 crushed
500 g (1 lb 2 oz) buffalo ricotta (or cow's milk ricotta)
Grated nutmeg, to taste
250 g (9 oz) minced buffalo or beef
Finely grated parmesan, to serve

Pasta dough

400 g (14 oz/2⅔ cups) pasta ("00") flour or plain (all-purpose) flour, plus extra for dusting
4 eggs, beaten

Sage butter sauce

125 g (4½ oz) butter
1 tablespoon extra-virgin olive oil
1 handful sage leaves, coarsely chopped
1 handful rosemary leaves, coarsely chopped
1 garlic clove, crushed

To make the dough, mix flour, eggs and a large pinch of salt together in a bowl, then knead for 10 minutes until dough springs back easily. Add extra flour or water as needed. Wrap dough in plastic wrap and rest at room temperature for 30 minutes.

Blanch silverbeet in a large saucepan of boiling salted water with a splash of olive oil and 1 garlic clove for 2–3 minutes or until soft. Drain well, then chop very finely — you should have about 250 g (9 oz). Combine with half the ricotta and a pinch of nutmeg.

Heat 1 tablespoon oil in a large frying pan over medium–high heat. Add mince and crushed garlic, season with salt and pepper, and fry, stirring occasionally, for 10–12 minutes until browned. Cool, then combine with remaining ricotta and a pinch of nutmeg.

Cut off a quarter of the dough, dust it with flour and roll out on a lightly floured surface to 3 mm (⅛ in) thick. Alternatively, use a pasta roller, starting on the widest setting and reducing settings notch by notch until 3 mm (⅛ in) thick (dust with flour as you go). Place small dollops of filling in a line along the sheet, 5 cm (2 in) apart and slightly off-centre. Brush edges with a wet finger, then fold pasta over, pushing out any air. Cut into squares, then seal with your fingers. Place on a floured surface and repeat with remaining dough and fillings.

For the sauce, combine butter and oil in a frying pan over low–medium heat. Add herbs and garlic, season, and cook, swirling occasionally, for 5 minutes or until herbs are just starting to crisp.

Meanwhile, cook ravioli in batches in a large saucepan of boiling salted water for 2 minutes or until al dente. Toss in sage butter sauce and serve topped with parmesan and olive oil.

Jacqui's pig's head terrine

'You'd be hard pressed to find an early Australian cookbook that doesn't include good old-fashioned brawn, but when was the last time you saw an animal's head at the butcher's shop? Enter Feather and Bone. Brawn is finding its way back onto menus as *pâté de tête* or "head cheese" and is a dish worth reviving, turning what's often a waste product into a delicious way to maintain our food heritage.'

Jacqui Newling, retail customer

———

Feeds: 8+ on a charcuterie board
Preparation time: 1 hour 10 minutes, plus 6 hours setting | Cooking time: 4 hours
Special equipment: A terrine mould, muslin (cheesecloth), kitchen string

1 pig's head, cut in half through the centre, brined for 24 hours (ask your butcher to do this)
4 pig's trotters, brined for 24 hours (ask your butcher to do this)
3 large celery stalks, cut into 5 cm lengths
3 large carrots, cut into large pieces
1 small bunch flat-leaf parsley, leaves and stalks reserved separately
2 bay leaves
1 large brown onion, trimmed
4 cloves
1 tablespoon black peppercorns
1 teaspoon allspice berries
3 blades of mace, or ½ teaspoon freshly grated nutmeg
1 teaspoon juniper berries
3 tablespoons apple cider vinegar
½ teaspoon savoury quatre épices (available from select delicatessens; or substitute with ½ teaspoon ground white pepper and a pinch each of ground nutmeg, ginger and cloves)
Baby cornichons, wholemeal toast and crisp salad leaves, to serve

Rinse head and trotters, place them in a large saucepan and cover with water. Add celery, carrot and parsley stalks. 'Nail' bay leaves to onion with cloves and add it to the pan. Tie remaining spices into a piece of muslin with kitchen string. Bring to the boil, then reduce heat to low and simmer, skimming every so often, for 3 hours or until the meat comes away easily from the bones. Cool briefly, then remove and discard vegetables and spices, and transfer the pork to a large bowl.

Strain the liquor into a clean saucepan, bring to the boil, and boil for 20–30 minutes or until reduced by half. Strain through a fine sieve, add vinegar and quatre épices and season to taste with salt.

Meanwhile, line a 1.5 litre (52 fl oz/6 cup) terrine mould, loaf tin or decorative mould with plastic wrap.

Use your hands to pull all the meat off the head and trotters, discarding the skin. Break or cut cheek and jowl meat into small pieces but not so small that they lose their character. Peel and discard skin from the tongue, then thinly slice it and the ears and break up the meat from the snout. Gently mingle the parts together.

To assemble, arrange some parsley leaves in the base of the mould. (If desired, chop any remaining leaves and mix them through the meat.) Fill the mould with the meat, gently pressing it down, then pour in the stock to just cover — tilt the mould gently to make sure it has filled any gaps. Cover with plastic wrap and refrigerate for 6 hours or overnight until the stock has set into aspic (jelly).

Uncover and invert the mould onto a plate and remove the plastic wrap. Serve in thin slices with cornichons, toast and salad leaves.

Feather and Bone's cassoulet

If you haven't tried it, cassoulet is the kind of dish that makes the cook appear fabulously brilliant and everyone who eats it feel brilliantly fabulous. A slow-cooked peasant dish originating in the south of France and named after the earthenware pot in which it was traditionally cooked, cassoulet is a rich, nurturing, one-pot wonder of beans and meat that is delicious in winter, but just as good in warmer months with a crisp green salad and wine. The core ingredients usually include pork sausages, cured pork, confit duck and beans but there are at least as many variations as letters in the name and all are fiercely defended as THE correct cassoulet. All we know is that this is the one we've made for years now with great success, so we're sticking to it.

Feeds: 4–6 | Preparation time: 15 minutes | Cooking time: 1½–2 hours
Special equipment: A large heavy-based ovenproof saucepan with a lid, kitchen string

300 g (10½ oz) fresh, tinned or dried organic borlotti beans
30 g (1 oz) duck fat
1 brown onion, diced
2 garlic cloves, crushed
400 g (14 oz) smoked pork shoulder or speck
4 lamb shoulder chops (about 100 g/3½ oz each)
500 ml (17 fl oz/2 cups) duck or chicken stock
2 confit duck Marylands (from select delicatessens)
4 Toulouse sausages (or substitute good-quality pastured pork sausages)
1 bunch Dutch carrots, trimmed and scrubbed
400 g (14 oz) tinned chopped tomatoes
Bouquet garni (sprigs of parsley, thyme, sage and bay leaves tied together with kitchen string in a small bunch)
60 g (2¼ oz/1 cup) sourdough breadcrumbs made from day-old bread
1 handful flat-leaf parsley leaves, coarsely chopped
Leafy green salad, to serve

If using dried borlotti beans, soak them in cold water overnight. Rinse, transfer to a saucepan and top with cold water, then bring to the boil, reduce heat to medium–low and simmer for 45 minutes or until they start to soften. Cool and refrigerate until needed.

Preheat oven to 150°C (300°F). In a large heavy-based ovenproof saucepan with a lid, melt 2 tablespoons duck fat over medium–low heat. Add onion and garlic and cook, stirring occasionally, for 5 minutes or until soft and just starting to colour. Add smoked pork or speck and cook, stirring, for another 2 minutes until slightly softened. Remove mixture from pan and set aside.

Increase heat to high, season lamb with salt and freshly ground black pepper, and fry, turning halfway, for 5 minutes or until browned on both sides. Add onion mixture, stock, confit duck, sausages, carrots, tomatoes and bouquet garni. Stir to combine, season well with salt and pepper, and top with beans. The contents should be just covered with liquid — if not, add a little water. Add half the breadcrumbs, then cover with a lid and bake for 1½–2 hours or until beans are cooked and lamb is completely tender and pulls easily away from the bone.

Remove the lid, toss remaining breadcrumbs with parsley and scatter on top. Bake for 15 minutes or until breadcrumbs are golden. Serve with a crisp, green leafy salad.

Ye olde mincemeat pies

'Once upon a time, "meat" referred to food generally, not just animal flesh, and "mincemeat" was a mixture of suet, meat, dried fruit, distilled spirits and spices. Those rich, spicy flavours we associate with the mince pies we tuck into at Christmas arrived in the 13th century with crusaders returning from the Middle East and bringing new spices and recipes. In more recent history, mincemeat fell out of favour until, in Victorian-era Britain, someone decided it was fashionable again and revived the tradition of eating mincemeat pies at Christmas. This was "special occasion" food containing all the rich, extravagant ingredients that you couldn't afford on a regular basis, including meat, and it would have been the height of luxury at the time. Still is, we reckon. Over time, the mincemeat pie was adapted and sweetened and became more like a dessert and finally forgot its namesake ingredient altogether. We've put the meat back in.

A real mincemeat pie, like beef and wine, needs to be aged to deepen the flavours and allow the preservative action of the alcohol, which gradually changes the overall texture of the mixture by breaking down the meat proteins. Apparently, preserved mincemeat may be stored for up to 10 years. Three to four weeks is enough for us.

Start this recipe at least a month before you intend to eat your mincemeat pies. You can make the pastry ahead and freeze it or make it on the day you're planning to cook your pies.'

Feather and Bone, Nonie Dwyer and Brent Templeton

———

Feeds: Makes around 20 pies | Mincemeat preparation time: 1 hr
Mincemeat ageing time: 3–4 weeks | Pastry preparation time: 30 minutes
Cooking time: 25 minutes | Special equipment: 20 small pie tins or pastry bases
and cookie cutter shapes if you want to add a decoration to the top of your pies

Finely grated zest and juice of 1 lemon
Finely grated zest and juice of 1 orange
1 Granny Smith apple
100 g (3½ oz) mixed peel
100 g (3½ oz) raisins, coarsely chopped
   to the same size as the mixed peel
100 g (3½ oz/⅔ cup) currants
50 g (1¾ oz/⅓ cup) cranberries,
   coarsely chopped to the same size
   as the mixed peel
50 g (1¾ oz/¼ cup) glacé ginger,
   coarsely chopped to the same size
   as the mixed peel
50 g (1¾ oz/¼ cup firmly packed)
   rapadura (or brown) sugar
50 g (1¾ oz/½ cup) almond meal
2 teaspoons ground cinnamon
2 teaspoons ground nutmeg
1 teaspoon ground cloves
100 g (3¾ oz) suet (order from
   your butcher)
200 g (7 oz) minced beef
100 ml (3½ fl oz) port or brandy
Butter, for greasing

Pastry

350 g (12 oz) butter, cut into 2–3 cm
   (¾–¼ in) dice, plus extra for greasing
500 g (1 lb 2 oz/3⅓ cups) plain (all-
   purpose) flour, plus extra for dusting
75 g (2¾ oz/⅓ cup firmly packed)
   rapadura (or brown) sugar
1 egg
Milk, for brushing

Place citrus juice and zest in a bowl. Peel apple (reserve peel) and grate flesh into the juice, making sure it gets coated in juice to stop it from browning. Add mixed peel, raisins, currants, cranberries and ginger, toss to coat, then add sugar, almond meal, spices, 1 teaspoon salt and 1 teaspoon freshly ground black pepper and mix well.

Melt suet in a frying pan over medium heat, then add mince. Cook slowly, stirring constantly to break up the meat and prevent clumping, for 10–15 minutes or until browned. Reduce heat to very low, add fruit mixture, stir to combine and cook, covered and stirring regularly, for 30–40 minutes until fruit is soft and plump and everything is well combined.

Cool to room temperature, then add port or brandy and mix thoroughly. Cover with plastic wrap and refrigerate for 3–4 weeks to let the flavours develop, much like a Christmas fruitcake. The meat will be preserved by the sugar and alcohol.

To make the pastry, on a clean work surface, chop butter through the flour and sugar with a pastry card (or blitz in a food processor) until it resembles small pebbles. Whisk egg with 75 ml (2½ fl oz) water. Pour onto flour mix and chop through by hand until it just comes together into a rough dough. Knead it a little to bring it together if necessary. Shape into a block, wrap in plastic wrap and chill.

Remove pastry from fridge and allow it to become pliable but not soft. Roll pastry out on a lightly floured surface to about 3 mm (⅛ in) thick. Cut into rounds large enough to line your pie tins — these are your pastry bases and tops. Use a decorative pastry cutter to cut out any decorative shapes from the tops.

Grease pie tins with butter, line them with pastry bases, then fill them generously with the pie filling. Brush the pastry tops and decorations with a little milk and press them onto the pies, using the decorative pieces for some, and the cutouts for others. Chill. Preheat oven to 180°C (350°F), then bake pies straight from the fridge for 20–25 minutes or until the pastry is golden brown. Serve warm or at room temperature.

Chris's whole, marinated, spit-roasted lamb

Chris's father had been a motorbike courier from Argos, and he first learned how to cook spits when he did his two years of national service in the Greek army. When his Commander discovered Chris's father was from Argos, an area famous for spit-roasted lamb, he immediately put him in charge of cooking the lambs to feed several hundred troops for their annual Easter feast. Despite never having cooked a lamb before, Chris's father found himself overseeing 40–50 manually turned spits with the Commander expecting a tremendous result. As he told Chris, there was no room for error — and so he became an overnight expert.

When his father died, Chris took over the role of Easter spit-master, continuing the family tradition of stuffing the lamb with his father's special recipe and cooking and carving for the extended family celebration. The rest of the family also maintain their tradition of reassuring Chris that they'll be there early to help, then turning up 10 minutes before the lamb is ready to eat. Chris has been delighting us and our customers for years and if he ever moves to Greece we will miss him dearly.

Chris Kottras, spit-master and retail customer

———

Makes: Depends on the size of the lamb; a 22 kg lamb will feed about 45 people
Preparation time: About 30 minutes — make the marinade the previous day, the longer the flavours mix, the better
Cooking time: 14–18 kg (31 lb–40 lb), 5 hours; 18–20 kg (40 lb–44 lb), 5½ hours; 20–25 kg (44 lb–55 lb), 6 hours; 25 kg (55 lb) or more, 6 hours+
Special equipment: A spit, charcoal, kitchen string, needle, thin wire and pliers

10 lemons, juiced, skins reserved,
   plus 1 extra
Around 600 ml (20 fl oz/2½ cups) extra-
   virgin olive oil, plus extra for drizzling
2 garlic bulbs
1 bunch dried Greek oregano (from
   select delicatessens)
1 teaspoon hot paprika
1 whole lamb (order from your butcher)
400 g (14 oz) kefalograviera (or another
   hard sheep's milk cheese or a mixture of
   sheep's and goat's milk cheeses), half
   diced, half cut into thin strips
2 long red chillies, halved lengthways

Begin this recipe a day ahead. To make the basting marinade, measure the amount of juice the lemons yield, then pour the juice into a mixing bowl and add half the quantity of olive oil — for example, for 500 ml (17 fl oz/2 cups) lemon juice, add 250 ml (9 fl oz/1 cup) oil. Mince the cloves from 1 garlic bulb and add them to the bowl. Rub dried oregano between your hands so the leaves fall into the bowl and you're left with the stalks. Keep the stalks; they'll go into the lamb tomorrow along with the lemon skins. Add paprika and season to taste with salt and freshly ground black pepper. Combine well, then cover and refrigerate overnight.

Recipe continued over page

→

For as long as he can remember, Chris Kottaras' father would drag Chris out of bed early on Easter Sunday to help stuff and roast the celebratory lamb for the clan and pass on the secret Greek business of perfect spit roasting.

Let's eat

The day of cooking, set coals up in the spit — put a small pile at either end of the fire pit; you're aiming for greater heat on the legs and shoulders and less heat on the belly. Light the coals about 45 minutes before you're planning to put the lamb on so they have plenty of time to settle into a moderate, even heat — you want to start cooking your lamb slowly. When you light the coals, bring the lamb to room temperature — never cook with cold meat.

Secure the lamb on the spit pole and place it on a table ready for stuffing. Cut thin holes into the legs and shoulders, cut 6 garlic cloves into strips, and stuff them into the holes with the kefalograviera strips — these will flavour the lamb as it cooks.

Combine remaining garlic (about 6 cloves; keep these whole) with diced kefalograviera, chilli, reserved lemon skins, oregano stalks and a splash of oil. Season to taste, then use this mixture to stuff the lamb cavity. Sew the cavity closed with kitchen string and a needle and close up the chest cavity with some thin wire.

Check that the lamb is safely secured to the spit pole — tie all four legs and neck to the spit pole to keep it all together as it cooks. Place the pole on the spit and start cooking, maintaining a low heat at the beginning. As the cooking progresses, slowly increase the heat.

About 90 minutes in, you should see the lamb fat start to render out. When you see this, sprinkle the lamb liberally with salt to draw out the fat. At this point, fetch the basting marinade and let it come to room temperature.

About 3 hours into cooking, cut a lemon in half, dip it into the marinade so it soaks up the liquid, then use the lemon to baste the lamb. Continue basting the lamb with the lemon dipped in marinade every 30 minutes until the lamb is golden, crisp and tender and the core temperature in legs and shoulders is maintained for at least 90 to 120 minutes.

When cooked, most of the meat can be readily stripped from the bones by hand (wear a double layer of food-handling gloves). Discard sinew, excess fat and membrane as you go. You may need a boning knife to get all of the leg meat off the bone. Keep meat warm in a large metal tray positioned near the leftover coals.

Our guiding principles — established in 2006

- We do our best to offer as much information as we can about the production, treatment, transport and preparation of our produce.

- We aim to supply exceptional produce sourced directly from producers throughout New South Wales, and occasionally beyond.

- We don't buy from third parties and we guarantee the provenance of all produce sold under our name.

- We seek out, and give preference to, producers working with rare and endangered breeds of livestock, with specific attention to rare breeds of pigs, cattle, sheep and poultry.

- All animals sold by us have been raised predominantly outside, which doesn't mean simply having 'access' to the sun, fresh air and water, but in a situation where the animal is substantially free to express instinctive behaviours.

- No product carried by us has been administered growth promotants at any point in its life. Antibiotics are only used where absolutely necessary and are not part of the routine diet of any animal we source.

- Similarly, with pasture management, chemical fertilisers are used sparingly, if at all, and strong preference is given to producers utilising various natural systems for promoting plant and ecosystem diversity and improving soil health and fertility.

- Occasionally it may be necessary to use grain as part of a ruminant's diet but no cow, sheep or goat sourced by us is the product of a continuous grain-fed regime.

- We only source whole animals that arrive entire, neither boxed nor packed in plastic. (If the producer themselves also breaks and butchers their own produce, we may then buy the parts they have for sale directly from them.)

- Every attempt is made by our producers to practice low stress stock handling throughout the growth cycle and at slaughter. Occasionally errant abattoir and/or transport practices can undermine the best practice of the producers and this will be reflected in the quality of the meat. We strive to minimise this through close liaison with transport and processing facilities.

- We dry-age our meat on the bone for 1–8 weeks. For delivery purposes use is made of loose bags or vacuum packaging but extended storage in plastic is always avoided.

- We endeavour to make all of our processes as transparent as possible. Enquiries regarding any and all aspects of production are welcome as are visits to our production facility.

Acknowledgements

A book like this is only possible because we are fortunate to operate at the intersection of a diverse and wonderful community, each member with their own influence, both subtle and profound, and each as important as the other.

As we have argued repeatedly, while there isn't really a beginning or an end when it comes to food production, consumption and responsibility, for us it all starts at the farm, and this book (and our business) is made possible by those who believe their farm can be a riot of productive capacity and are willing to share a small, but crucial, part with us. We've lost count, but over the years we've been hosted at more than a hundred farms scattered over many thousands of kilometres across five states. To all those people who have put us up and/or put up with us, either singly, or as a roaming staff or family pack, and who have trusted and befriended and taught us, we can't thank you enough. We can only hope we have faithfully reflected your passion, conveyed a small fragment of your knowledge and done your fine produce justice.

It may start on the farm but it finishes on the table. It was our customers' insistent curiosity and inspiring determination to take greater control over their food choices that first got us thinking that writing a book that answered their daily questions might be a useful thing to do.

One of the joys of our work (and a source of constant delight) is how many of our community have become our friends. From farmers and customers whose children we've watched grow up through to those who've moved on, to chefs ordering every other day for their restaurants through to our once-a-year Christmas-ham customer; their ideas, support, feedback and friendship has made our work worthwhile. Everyone wants an appreciative audience. We are astounded how powerful that appreciation can be.

Of course, a business like ours is nothing without its staff. What started as a one-man band has expanded and over the years we have been blessed to work with many talented and wonderful people who have each made important contributions to Feather and Bone. To all of you, past and present, we give a huge thank you.

Then there are the unsung heroes behind the scenes that make this whole shebang function: the stock handlers, abattoir workers, meat carters and delivery drivers whose work is demanding and sometimes dangerous and exacts a physical and emotional toll that is mostly overlooked. They deserve our acknowledgement and gratitude.

Thanks to the team at Murdoch for skilfully navigating us through and trusting that this slightly awkward hybrid of polemic, exposition, photographs and recipes might find an audience. To Jane Morrow, thank you for keeping the faith and the door open for the four years it took us to finally commit to writing this book. To Justin Wolfers, we're so grateful for your skill, good humour and saintly patience in wrangling us and this project to conclusion. Huge thanks to photographer, Alan Benson, for the beautiful images, the endless support and more favours than we deserve, and for not fainting at the abattoir.

This book is the product of the trust and generosity of hundreds of producers, thousands of customers and millions of microbes. We can only hope that it adequately reflects those gifts, and truly demonstrates the power of food to connect people, plants and animals across space and time.

Finally, we thank our three beautiful sons — Gilbert, Ambrose and Louis. Our work is for your future.

Further reading

Books

Barber, Dan: *The Third Plate: Field Notes on the Future of Food* (Penguin Press, 2014)

Berry, Wendell: *Home Economics* (Counterpoint, 2009 [1987])

Blythman, Joanna: *Swallow This* (4th Estate, 2016)

Bromfield, Louis: *Pleasant Valley* (Wooster Book Company, 1997 [1946])

Brunetti, Jerry: *The Farm as Ecosystem* (Acres USA, 2014)

Chan, Gabrielle: *Rusted Off: Why Country Australia is Fed Up* (Penguin Random House, 2018)

Danforth, Adam: *Butchering Poultry, Rabbit, Lamb, Goat, Pork* (Storey Publishing, 2014); *Butchering Beef* (Storey Publishing, 2014)

Evans, Matthew: *On Eating Meat* (Murdoch Books, 2019)

Fairlie, Simon: *Meat: A Benign Extravagance* (Permanent Publications, 2011)

Fearnley-Whittingstall, Hugh: *The River Cottage Meat Book* (Ten Speed Press, 2007)

Hahn-Niman, Nicolette: *Righteous Porkchop* (William Morrow, 2016)

Hartley, Dorothy: *Food in England* (Little Brown, 2009 [1954])

Herzog, Hal: *Some We Love, Some We Hate, Some We Eat* (Harper Collins, 2011)

Imhoff, Daniel: *The CAFO Reader: The Tragedy of Industrial Animal Factories* (Earth Aware Editions, 2010)

Keith, Lierre: *The Vegetarian Myth: Food, Justice and Sustainability* (Flashpoint Press, 2009)

Massy, Charles: *Call of the Reed Warbler: a New Agriculture, a New Earth* (University of Queensland Press, 2017)

McGee, Harold: *McGee on Food and Cooking* (Hodder and Stoughton, 2004)

Miller, Daphne: *Farmacology: Total Health from the Ground Up* (William Morrow, 2016)

Monbiot, George: *Feral: Rewilding the Land, the Sea and Human Life* (University of Chicago Press, 2017)

Muir, Cameron: *The Broken Promise of Agricultural Progress: An Environmental History* (Routledge, 2014)

Newell, Patrice: *Who's Minding the Farm* (Viking Penguin, 2020)

Lymbery, Philip; Oakshott, Isabel: *Farmageddon: The True Cost of Cheap Meat* (Bloomsbury, 2017)

Pascoe, Bruce: *Dark Emu* (Magabala Books, 2018)

Patchirat, Timothy: *Every Twelve Seconds: Industrialised Slaughter and the Politics of Sight* (Yale University Press, 2013)

Pollan, Michael: *The Omnivore's Dilemma* (Penguin Press, 2017 [2006])

Pommeresche, Herwig: *Humusphere: Humus: A substance or a living system?* (Acres USA, 2019)

Provenza, Fred: *Nourishment: What Animals Can Teach Us About Rediscovering Our Natural Wisdom* (Chelsea Green, 2018)

Rebanks, James: *The Shepherd's Life* (Penguin Random House UK, 2016)

Rolls, Eric: *A Million Wild Acres* (Hale and Iremonger 2011 [1981])

Rose, Nick (Ed.): *Fair Food* (University of Queensland Press, 2015)

Safran Foer, Jonathan: *Eating Animals* (Penguin Books, 2013)

Salatin, Joel: *Fields of Farmers: Interning, Mentoring, Partnering Germinating* (Polyface, 2013)

Wallace, Charles: *Big Farms Make Big Flu* (Monthly Review Press, 2016)

Walters, Charles; Fry, Gerald: *Reproduction and Animal Health* (Acres USA, 2003)

Watson, Don: *The Bush* (Penguin Books, 2017)

Websites / blogs

Acres USA: Tractor Time Podcast
acresusa.com/pages/tractor-time-podcast

Australian Food Sovereignty Alliance
afsa.org.au/

Civil Eats
civileats.com/

Compassion in World Farming
ciwf.org.uk/

Food and Agriculture Organisation of the United Nations
fao.org/home/en/

Grist — food
grist.org/food/

Mother Jones — food
motherjones.com/food/

Slow Food Foundation for Biodiversity
fondazioneslowfood.com/en/

Sustainable Food Trust
sustainablefoodtrust.org/

The Counter
thecounter.org/

The Nature Conservancy
nature.org/en-us

Index

Published in 2020 by Murdoch Books, an imprint of Allen & Unwin

Murdoch Books Australia
83 Alexander Street
Crows Nest NSW 2065
Phone: +61 (0)2 8425 0100
murdochbooks.com.au
info@murdochbooks.com.au

Murdoch Books UK
Ormond House, 26–27 Boswell Street
London WC1N 3JZ
Phone: +44 (0) 20 8785 5995
murdochbooks.co.uk
info@murdochbooks.co.uk

For corporate orders and custom publishing, contact our business
development team at salesenquiries@murdochbooks.com.au

Publisher: Jane Morrow
Editorial Manager: Justin Wolfers
Design Manager: Megan Pigott
Designer: Murray Batten
Recipe editor: David Matthews
Narrative editor: Katri Hilden
Photographer: Alan Benson
Stylist: Emma Knowles
Home Economist: Wilson Chung
Production Director: Lou Playfair

ISBN 978 1 76052 455 5 Australia
ISBN 978 1 91163 270 2 UK

A catalogue record for this
book is available from the
National Library of Australia

A catalogue record for this book is available from the British Library

Colour reproduction by Splitting Image Colour Studio Pty Ltd, Clayton, Victoria
Printed by C & C Offset Printing Co. Ltd., China

TABLESPOON MEASURES: We have used 20 ml (4 teaspoon) tablespoon measures. If you are using a
15 ml (3 teaspoon) tablespoon add an extra teaspoon of the ingredient for each tablespoon specified.

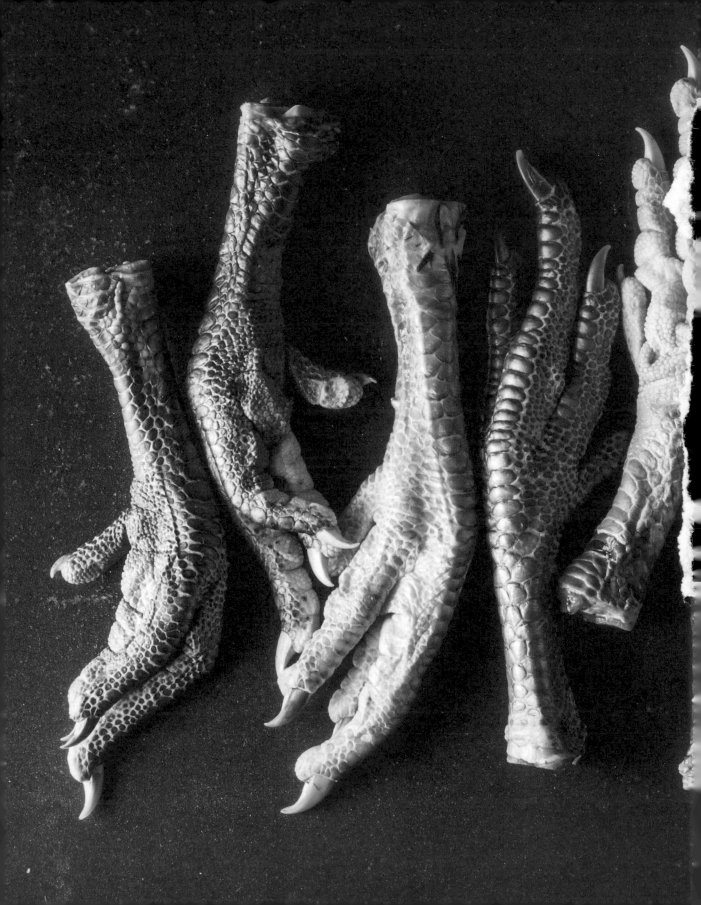